# Memories from New Hampshire's Lakes and Mountains

## Fence Building & Apple Cider

# Memories from New Hampshire's Lakes and Mountains

Bruce D. Heald

Published by The History Press
Charleston, SC 29403
www.historypress.net



*Front cover*: The Pemigewasset River and valley looking north to the Franconia Mountains from West Campton in the White Mountains.
*Back Cover*: The old mill and log cabin on Lake Kanasatka, Mountonboro, New Hampshire. *Drawing by William H. Bartlett, c. 1834.*

First published 2007

Manufactured in the United States

ISBN 978.1.59629.266.6

Library of Congress Cataloging-in-Publication Data

Heald, Bruce D., 1935–
Memories from New Hampshire's lakes and mountains : fence building and apple cider / Bruce D. Heald.
p. cm.
Includes bibliographical references.
ISBN 978-1-59629-266-6 (alk. paper)
1. New Hampshire--Social life and customs. 2. Country life--New Hampshire. 3. City and town life--New Hampshire. 4. New Hampshire--History, Local. 5. Villages--New Hampshire. 6. Lakes--New Hampshire. 7. Mountains--New Hampshire. 8. Seasons--New Hampshire. I. Title.
F40.H43 2007
974.200973'4--dc22
2007018232

*Notice*: The information in this book is true and complete to the best of our knowledge. It is offered without guarantee on the part of the author or The History Press. The author and The History Press disclaim all liability in connection with the use of this book.

# Contents

# Acknowledgements

Special thanks to Richard Allen, Polly Ayre, Stephen Bennett, A.J. Downing, Timothy Dwight, Ralph W. Emerson, Enhanced Computers, J.S. Crane, John Flanders, Sam W. Foss, Watson Glider, Starr King, R.J. McGinnis, Kathy Melanson, Arthur Page, Theodore Parker, John Spargo, Charles Robinson, William F. Robinson, Frederick Tudor, Patricia Welch and John G. Whittier.

# Introduction

When we look at the early settlers of New Hampshire, we see a people of courage; an infinite drive and determination to succeed; a freedom of adventure; the challenge of abandoning the old for the new; the lure of an ever-receding frontier; and the restless movement in search of fulfilled life—a search for identity, individualism and freedom.

Now we have a new people in a new frontier where they had to be self-sufficient—to place a trade. Thus, the early settlers bonded together and built a community—the church, school, the country store, blacksmith shop all clustered around the village common.

The village became the focal point for many social, political and economic affairs where the farmers would gather together and bond their settlement and government as a family—"The Spirit of the Covenant."

Looking back on the early farm and family, there was a sense of peace, trust and security. It was a time when the community planted and harvested their crops. The farmer needed little from anybody or anything outside the limits of his own home. He built his own house, raised his own cattle, cared for his own fields and barn, the animals and the simple tools of the farmer's trade. His wife, in turn, cared for the home and provided nourishment and clothing for the family. There was the warm kitchen, perfumed with the aroma of fresh-baked bread.

This book describes some of the special memories of life on the New Hampshire farm, family and community of our past. It is a history of ordinary people as they once lived in their isolation and self-sufficiency. It is the intent of the author to preserve these memories before they are overlooked and soon forgotten. Let us cherish the special moments and events that celebrated their adventure and preserve it in memory.

## Chapter One

# Special Events

Special events are beautiful memories, especially for the young folk during years past. We do have some of the same events today—like a Christmas feast, Thanksgiving dinner and the church supper. However, some of the luster has left the good old days and the spirit of these events. During the old days, special events were rare, and something to look forward to with excitement and anticipation; we dreamt about them and saved our money because the more special the event, the more money it took.

A special event had to have a degree of regularity so that you knew what was coming and what to expect. A good example was Christmas, which was the most special event, but the country fair was a close second.

It was lucky that special events almost always came just when you needed them most. The fair came after harvest, the Fourth of July when you were all worn out with weeding the garden.

Kids could also have fun at family reunions and in the Christmas program at school. You got an orange as your treat after the program, and the orange was indeed a treasure. Grown-ups regarded the camp meeting and the revival at the village church as special events.

Of course there was Thanksgiving, when all the kinfolk got together for a big dinner, and Easter, when the women got new bonnets and the young folk had an egg hunt.

The circus was a very special event, and it was more fun for both the young and old than anything, but you never could depend on it. It was usually performed in the big city and it cost a lot of money for the whole family to go. You got up early in the morning and drove several miles to the city and you returned after dark with the chores to do.

Even a birthday, a new pup and your first long pants were special events. Parents regarded the arrival of a new baby as a very special event, but it bored the kids.

The more special events you had, the less you enjoyed them and some of them were not very exciting when you grew up. For example, Christmas was not nearly as much fun if you didn't believe in Santa Claus. But you never got tired of the country fair, and while you often wished it would last a year instead of three days, you knew very well you would get fed up with its thrills, as kids do now with special events happening every day.

## A Mountain Sanctuary

Many consider the mountains and the open country "land of the heart." It is the breathtaking space of short vacations furnished with a foundation upon which to build plans and schemes for future holidays in our mountainous region.

To some it consists of fond memories of old, well-known and beloved fields where they can bask in the warm country sunshine or linger in the cool shadows of some mountain glen, with the perpetual music of its rushing stream to lull the senses to blissful forgetfulness of present surroundings.

Then again, the mind may ramble on the most unusual, grandest and most glorious of prospects that we may ever have been fortunate enough to look upon, once more to visualize these inspirations to the sublime emotions.

Many of us have the pleasure of pure imagination to console us in the long winters of our discontent. Dreams we have of the places not yet visited and, sweetest of all, of those discovered by our own ingenuity of reading, and poring over maps, or places not known to fame but promising prospects. What enjoyment it is to keep a mental catalogue of such spots, to be ever on the alert for opportunities to learn more of them, to light on some reference to one of them in a book or periodic article.

These are all sanctuaries for the soul, but the most precious of all is the region of which we know something, the fringes of it possibly, yet over which the light of the imagination has full play. We know its character well enough to love it, and assuredly in advance, and because it contains no roadways, we know it is unspoiled. It is just as it was—a wilderness, an abandoned farm, a quiet, secluded waterfall in the hills of New Hampshire.

## A New Hampshire Tribute

"Let me live in a house by the side of the road where the race of men go by," wrote the New Hampshire poet Sam W. Foss. Nowhere could he find a finer class of men than in his native state.

New Hampshire knew the youth of Daniel Webster, of Horace Greeley and Charles A. Dana, of our fourteenth president, Franklin Pierce, and of General Leonard Wood.

The sculptor Augustus Saint-Gaudens lived and worked in this state. The memory of the composer Edward MacDowell is honored by the books, plays and music that pour forth from Peterboro; the Cornish colony is noted in the world of arts and letters. Here the philosopher William James wandered contentedly in the foothills of Mount Chocorua, and here Whittier and Robert Frost and many other poets have found inspiration for their pen in the lakes and mountains of New Hampshire.

Four great New England rivers have their source in New Hampshire—the Saco and the Merrimack, the Connecticut and the rushing Androscoggin turned the wheels of industry during the late nineteenth and early twentieth centuries. New Hampshire textile and blankets, boots and shoes and paper and wood products were known the world over. Her granite monoliths grace our buildings; her potatoes, peaches, apples and maple sugar delight our tongues.

Proud is New Hampshire of Dartmouth, that college sprung from Eleazar Wheelock's determination "to spread Christian knowledge among the savages of our American wilderness." She honors Exeter and St. Paul's and her flourishing University of New Hampshire at Durham, Plymouth and Keene.

Our state rejoices in the mountain ranges and cool blue lakes and the bracing, healthful air that draws thousands of summer and winter visitors across her welcoming borders.

Join the joyous procession. Drive through the White Mountains. Ride America's oldest cogwheel railroad to the summit of Mount

A majestic view of Lake Winnipesaukee and the village of Center Harbor. *Etched by William H. Bartlett, 1834.*

Washington. Linger in the Flume at Franconia Notch, and etch Echo Lake with its memories of the Old Man of the Mountain. See the navy yard at Portsmouth, where John Paul Jones equipped the Rangers; and the wild and curious Isles of Shoals off the New Hampshire coast; or camp on the shores of Lake Winnipesaukee, Squam Lake, Ossipee or Sunapee Lakes. Their musical Native American names give constant witness that here lived and loved another group of people.

What better way to celebrate life than to live and embrace it with the beauty of our lakes and mountains.

## NEW HAMPSHIRE'S PINE TREES

Our neighboring state of Maine enjoys the proud distinction of being the pine tree state, yet her pines are no friendlier than can be found in New Hampshire, nor is the pine any more characteristic of her soil. In fact, her honor is one that we thoughtlessly let fall from our hands, for during the early days of settlement, we were called the pine tree colony. Our flag had a pine for its symbol, and when John Paul Jones sailed out from Portsmouth to whip the British navy, he carried at his masthead "the pine tree flag." In the middle of the eighteenth century, the British king ordered all pines in New Hampshire over 160 feet in height blazed and preserved for masts in "His Majesty's navy."

For many years I have camped in the wilderness areas of the White Mountains. I have come to appreciate the friendliness of the pine tree and to see how splendid a gift God gave us when he gave us a state covered with the gigantic pines that the early settlers found, along with the more intimate and companionable smaller pines. The white pine of New England is considered the friendliest, most beautiful and most useful tree that grows upon the earth. If grown in an open place, the pine becomes a beautiful and gracefully thick green spire. If grown in thick lots, it becomes a tall, dignified parasol. If let out on a bleak hill by itself, it becomes the rugged bull pine. Wherever it grows, it is always beautiful; it is always a shelter for life. Its branches run out straight from its trunk in a horizontal position, giving a thick and extended shade and shelter beneath. Its dropping needles make the most exquisite carpet that nature provides. Under such protecting arms, birds, squirrels, rabbits and smaller animals are delighted to nestle and make it their home. The squirrel feeding on the cones above, the hare and chipmunk digging among the roots, the birds chirping among the branches—and here I camp beneath, testifying to the delights of the pine trees. Nature seems to have designed this tree, above all others, to be the shelter and protector of animal life.

The treatment of the pine in the writings of mankind is evidence to what I proclaim. No tree has created so deep and lasting emotion as the pine. Literature is the expression of man's innermost personality, and in the literature of the world is abundant evidence of the feeling of man for the pine tree. Turning to the poets, we find the pine tree celebrated.

To reflect these literary passages of the earlier writers, I present the following:

*Sweet are the whispers of yon pine*
*That makes low music o're the spring.*

On the grounds of Camp Pineland stood the majestic Whittier pine, associated with the Quaker poet John Greenleaf Whittier. Sitting beneath the branches and looking to vistas of Squam Lake and the foothill of the White Mountains, Whittier composed "Summer by the Lakeside," "The Wood Giant," "Storm on Lake Asquam" and "The Hill-top."

So sang Theocritus, the first of the writers to appreciate nature's design.

"'Neath a waving sea of gentle pines" is a line in *Horace* that expressed what so many have noted, that the pine woodlands in both sight and sound are verily like the majestic ocean. One may appreciate this after climbing a little and looking down upon a waving sea of pine tops.

As the white pine is the glory of the spies, we may well expect that American writers will pay the best tributes, and we are not disappointed. Longfellow likes the "pine groves with soft and soul-like sounds." He speaks of the "sea-suggesting pines," and reaches the apex of his treatment in the poem "My Cathedral."

Lowell speaks of the pine but thinks it melancholy. Whittier, of course, loved the pines, but felt something like Lowell. In his love sonnet, Theodore Parker, that many-sided intellectual giant, pays a fine tribute to the pine when he writes, "My love is pure, like a pine-tree is a waste of snow." Burroughs has a fine essay on "the spray of pine" and Watson Glider tells us what a fine place for a camp is in a pine grove. But the greatest lovers of the pine are the great Concord pair, Emerson and

Thoreau. Thoreau tells us the pine points straight to heaven; however, he had a lasting quarrel with the timid Lowell, who cuts out his statement that the pine tree is immortal and will go as high as man.

Emerson tells us the pine trees talked to him and were inspirations of his philosophy. His stately Concord home was beneath a ground of pines that murmured their music into the room where he spent his mornings with his books. And it was under the half-grown pines at Canterbury where he loved to lie and brood and from whence he hurls his defiance at the world to disturb him, when he writes:

*O, when I am stretched beneath the pines,*
*Where the evening star so holy shines,*
*I laugh at the lore and pride of man.*

With this age-old joy in the pines of the wilderness and the celebration of its delights by the writers of this land, such as John G. Whittier of Center Harbor, it is no wonder we feel the grace of heaven can have no greater joys than come to us in the majesty of New Hampshire.

## New England Weather

I'm no weather forecaster, but a native will tell you that the mention of New England weather brings to mind sayings like, "If you don't like the weather, wait a minute," and "What you see is what you get," or "We have two seasons—July and winter," or its variant, "Nine months of winter and three of rough sledding." The foreigners to New England may well wonder just what the local climate is really like.

The answer depends on what part of the region he or she is wondering about. Although New England is not large compared to other sections of the country, it suffers a fairly wide range of climate. For example, there is no dry season. Throughout the year, precipitation averages between three and four inches a month, although there are occasional months with five times that amount and others with none at all. During the spring and summer, the rainfall is about the same in New England as it is in the rest of the northeastern states. But whereas autumn and winter are substantially drier in other places, in New England the moisture keeps coming and on the average it rains, snows or sleets about one out of three days year round.

In spite of the abundant precipitation, there are about as many fine clear days as there are in most of the Southern states. In Connecticut, at least one day in three is bright and clear; northern Vermont and New Hampshire have substantially fewer days like this.

On days that are warm and sunny everywhere else, fog may lie chill and damp along the seacoast, especially from Cape Cod northward. Thick fog may form in the inland valleys, especially in May and September when noondays are warm and nights are chilly. This type of fog materializes out of thin, clear air during the night and drips from trees and bushes all through the evening. The next morning, early risers know that if the fog lifts from below, it will come down again later as rain, but if it lies close to the ground, it will surely burn off from the top to make a fine day. On such a morning, hilltops emerge first into sunlight and the last foggy remnant may lie late in the valley below like a large white roll of insubstantial cotton.

The New England climate offers nothing so violent as a Kansas heat wave or a blizzard in the Rocky Mountains, but the weather fluctuates much more often within its lesser range of possibilities than it does in most other sections of North America. A glance at a map of storm tracks across the country shows part of the reason for this change. Our storms follow two main paths. One of these comes in from west to east across the Great Lakes; the other comes up from the South along the Atlantic Coast and both go out to sea over New England and the St. Lawrence Valley. Moreover, New England lies just athwart the zone where cold, dry air from the Arctic regions over Canada encounters warm, moist air moving up from over tropical seas. These two very different kinds of air masses are constantly moving back and forth, and when they collide, it surely sets up a great turbulence.

The resulting weather offers many variations on a basically constant pattern. One day the wind blows cool and dry out of the northwest and the air is so transparently crystalline that even a blade of grass stands out individually on the farthest hill. The next day may look and feel the same, but a weather-minded outdoorsman—noting that the wind is in the northeast and the sky brushed with the plumy mare's tail of cirrus clouds—darkly labels it a "weather breeder." Naturally, the barometer falls, and a day or two later there is a deluge of blowing rain from the east for at least three days—though not always so in the summer. Perhaps the wind shifts from northwest to southwest and the forecast is calling for fair and warm weather. This pleasant state may last several days,

An aerial view of the White Mountains with snow-capped Mount Washington and the Presidential Range in the center background. On the summit of Mount Washington, weather observers were housed in the so-called Signal Station, which remained on the summit until the Great Fire of 1908. Mount Washington is the highest mountain east of the Rocky Mountains and north of the Carolinas, rising to a height of 6,288 feet above sea level. In April of 1934, the highest wind velocity in the world was recorded on the summit of this mountain. The wind reached the speed of 231 miles per hour.

but eventually the fair and warm turns to hot and muggy and the rain clouds that shut out the oppressive sun come as a welcome relief. Even while it is still raining, we may feel our spirit and energy rise and fall with the barometer. We may keep a watchful eye on the western horizon off toward the east like an opening curtain to let the sun in on a newly washed land, rounding one more cycle in what the weather bureau describes as "a more or less regular succession of biweekly storms of snow or rain, with intervening two- or three-day periods of fair weather."

Summers may be considered moderate in New England. The hottest days usually reach ninety or ninety-five degrees, comparable to northern Wisconsin or the lower Colorado Mountains. After dark, swimming is practically unheard of, except by the young, and one may regret leaving home for the evening without taking a sweater or light jacket.

What is an old-fashioned New Hampshire winter like? Relatively few people who live in northern New England can expect it to be both long and cold. In January, the temperature averages lower then ten degrees, and on occasional evenings, it drops to thirty below zero. Many times snow covers the ground continuously from Thanksgiving to mid-April, and over eight feet of it usually falls during this time.

Snow is a factor to be dealt with all winter long. It has to be shoveled from walks and doorways and even from rooftops. In exceptionally snowy years, many an old barn slumps over on its side under the weight of it. Roads soon run through blue-white canyons whose walls grow higher and higher as the plows throw each new snowfall up on top of the last. Nowadays people are rarely snowed in, even for a short time, since highway crews are out with their powerful plows almost as the first flakes fall.

Soon, on the dim, gray morning after months of constant snow and ice, people in the North Country of New Hampshire waken with a vague sense of pleasant anticipation, wondering why the mood so poorly matches the sodden day.

The spring thaw in our North Country occurs when the bare soil appears through the slushy remnants and marks the beginning of the mud season. During the long winter, as snow piles up on the ground, the cold penetrates several feet down and freezes the moisture that is abundant in late autumn. Come spring, it takes several weeks for the frozen ground to thaw from the top down so that snowmelt, as well as newly falling rain, may drain away from below. Meanwhile, the thawing surface is an undrained, muddy morass.

Still, New England's weather rarely indulges in dramatic behavior. Normally, it is a thing of constantly changing details, each to be savored while it lasts—whether a snapping, starlit winter evening, a spring day of petulant showers swept with flashes of sunshine or a long, golden midsummer night such as only a spare, Northern land can produce.

Chapter Two

# The Early Farmhouse

Most everywhere in New Hampshire the first farmhouses were log, pine, clapboard and the like. The logs came from the first clearing, snaked to the site by ox or horse, notched and hoisted in place by sheer human muscle. The logs were caulked with clay and a fieldstone fireplace was erected at one end of a single room. The roof was carefully made of hand-split shingles. If a man had time, he hewed the logs square and fitted them closely.

The house was designed for shelter, not for comfort or elegance. The windows were small, without blinds or shutters. The fireplace was sufficiently spacious to receive logs of three or four feet in diameter, with an oven in the back and a flue nearly large enough to allow the ascent of a balloon. A person might literally sit in the chimney corner and study astronomy. All the cooking was done in the fireplace. Around it, also, gathered the family—often numbering six or twelve children—in the evenings and the cricket in the hearth kept company to their prattle. Thus with the hardships came the comforts of life, in the days "lang syne."

As the farmer found time from the eternal round of planting and harvesting, he built the needed outbuildings around his dwelling. First came the barn, with stalls for the family cow and horses, a mow for hay and perhaps a lean-to for his sheep. If, by good fortune, there was a field spring on the homestead, the cabin was built near it and a springhouse became one of the outbuildings. Then came the outhouse, a smokehouse for curing meat, a root cellar, a woodshed and an ash pit.

Near the barn were the corncrib, the granary, pens for calves and hogs, a machine (tool) shed and perhaps a shop.

The buildings kept pace with the farmer's affluence; the cabin was enlarged and faced with clapboards or replaced by brick or stone and roofed with slate. The log barn was replaced by a sawed lumber structure. There were many stalls and the mow was high.

The furniture was simple and useful, all made of the wood from the nearby forest. The pine, birch, cherry, walnut and curled maple wood were more frequently chosen by the cabinetmaker. Vessels of iron, copper and tin were used in cooking. The dressers, extending from floor to ceiling in the kitchen, contained the mugs, basins and plates of pewter, which shone upon the farmer's board at the time of meals. A writer from the *New Hampshire Patriot* has given the following recollection of the kind of life described above.

> *In 1815, Farmers hired their help for nine or ten dollars a month—some clothing and the rest cash. Carpenters' wages, one dollar a day; journeymen carpenters, fifteen dollars a month; an apprentices, to serve six or seven years, had ten dollars the first year, twenty the second, and so on, and to clothe themselves. Breakfast generally consisted of potatoes roasted in the ashes a "bannock" made of meal and water and baked on a maple chip set before the fire. Pork was plenty. If "hash" was had for breakfast, all ate from the platter, without plates or table-spread. Apprentices and farm boys had for supper a bowl of scalded milk and a brown crust, or bean porridge, or pop-robin. There was no such thing as tumblers, more were they asked if they would have tea or coffee; it was "Please pass the mug."*

The post of the housewife was not sinecure. She had charge of both the dairy and kitchen, besides spinning and weaving, sewing, knitting, washing and mending for the men folks. The best room, often called the square room, contained a bed, a bureau or desk or a chest of drawers, a clock and possibly a brass fire-set. Its walls were as naked of ornaments as that of a shaker. We are describing a period that antedates the advent of pictures, pianos, carpets, lace curtains and Venetian blinds. It was an age of simple manners, industrious habits and untarnished morals. Contentment, enjoyment and longevity were prominent characteristics of the age; the average age was seventy years. It deserves notice, also, that many of the provincial governors and Revolutionary officers of the

The Dolly Copp Homestead, Pinkham Notch, New Hampshire, 1938. The early homestead was a tight little community. Out of necessity it was designed to be self-sufficient. It consisted of the main house, outhouse, shed and barn.

state lived to extreme old age. Fevers and epidemics sometimes swept away some of the population, but consumption and neuralgia were then almost unknown. The people were generally quite healthy.

The community exerted its own social and economic pressures on the farm family, which found, as the twentieth century dawned, that their fields were no longer an island and the way of life no longer in their own hands. Life became more complex, but in many ways much easier. The farmer willingly traded his hernia for electric power, his self-sufficiency for a community of interdependence and the toil and hardship of the frontier for the comfort of an ordered economy. This is progress and the farm community now has become dependent upon the community outside the homestead.

## Old Homes

Did you ever stop to consider that some of the most fascinating landmarks in the Lakes Region are the number of old homes situated on the back roads? This is the silent evidence of the integrity with

This is the residence of J.S. Crane, Lake Village (Laconia), New Hampshire. This estate overlooks Paugus Bay with the White Mountains in the distance.

which their builders built, of the soundness of the wood they chose and of the painstaking care and respect—not only the respect they had for themselves, but also the respect their children had for property. These houses today are preserved with sound roofs and solid sills. This is not to say, however, that all these old homes in the region are sound, for you may drive for many miles in the hill country before finding a deserted cellar hole, or a house left alone, tumbling in like a leper.

Here in the North Country, set aside from the industry of the large cities, the rigor and stamina of the climate hardened the moral fiber of the early people. The life of the farmer was not easy. Ownership of the acreage entailed—in addition to raising crops—the eternal wrestling with granite rocks and boulders cast up by the never-ending frost of winter and the everlasting fight to keep the forest down in his tillable acres. The farmer stuck to his plow longer and his sons and grandsons followed him in his home, building on when new members of his family demanded more room and repairing the inroads that our Northern winter made, until later we see these old houses as monuments to their families and a joy to those who, while appreciative of modern conveniences, cherish these sign posts along our journey forward.

One old home, situated in Lake Village in a meadow where bees and butterflies found refuge in the solitude on hot August afternoons, is brought to mind. This estate overlooks Paugus Bay with the White Mountains framing the northern horizon.

From this vantage point, the Ossipee Mountains smile, and to the north, the horizon frames the Sandwich Mountain Range. Beside it, towering majestically, is a magnificent old elm, the likes of which have never been seen before.

After feasting on this vista, we enter the old home. Here, as outside, everything belongs. There is a great central chimney, serving three fireplaces; long rows of books beside the fire in the living room; and huge beds, which at night one must sink into for rest and sleep more restful than elsewhere. The gracious hostess replaces the drab old bricks in the fireplace with quartz crystals gathered in the fields about the house. During the evening hours, when the flames in the fireplaces leap upward in a thousand facets, surely no one could wish back the red bricks of the past.

Beyond the living room is the carriage shed, a part of the house where one might find some barn swallows flying, for they too belong. In the loft, a confine too small to permit its display, is a loom, remnant of the early days of home industry whose products were more than serviceable.

When winter comes, this house on the hill sparkles with a different radiance and when the snow comes, great flakes dance down from Whiteface Mountain, and are swept by the wind across the hill on an almost never-ending journey toward the sea.

These homes, like aged wine and fine antiques, grow in value, enhance the landscape.

## Kitchens of the 1800s

In many of the old houses built nearly two hundred years ago, there may have been two kitchens—the low studded and dark chamber located in the basement of a brick house and the cozy kitchen in the center of the farmhouse. The vast basement kitchen of colonial days, with its broad beams fringed with pendent ears of corn and dried meat, still held the place of home-factory in the old country home. However, the well-equipped, comfortable kitchen in the small farmhouse was considered the heart of the house, and when the lamps were lighted, the shutters closed and a great wood fire sent out a flickering glow, the room became irresistible to the family. The kitchen was some twenty feet square with windows recessed in the deep walls of the house and secured against cold and intrusion by folding paneled shutters, held firmly in place by wooden bars fitted into sockets halfway up the casement.

The fireplace, the glowing eye of the room, was the center of attraction. Although not of the generous dimensions of its colonial fire-runners, it easily held the hickory logs "once cut," ten cords of which were annually piled in the great barn adjoining the house, after being sawed and split by some itinerant wood-sawyer. In a leather apron-like strap—which when folded over the wood was lifted by its handles, one at each end in the manner of a carpet bar—supplies were brought in daily to fill the kitchen wood box. And to make sure that the fire would burn quickly, there was the bark pile in the barn, a good supply of which was always kept on hand.

On the crane in the fireplace was hung, besides the smaller kettle and the pot for boiling potatoes and the like, a great three-gallon water kettle with a long spout and faucet, from which hot water could always be drawn without tipping it. Heavy wrought-iron firedogs or andirons

The living room in Sunset Cottage, Camp Asquam in Center Harbor, New Hampshire. The fireplace, the glowing eye of the room, was the center of family activity.

stood beneath the crane with hook-like brackets on the back on which to place a temporary spit.

The pride of the old kitchen was the assembly of boilers and ovens with fireboxes beneath them on either side of the fireplace. First came the copper wash boiler with its individual firebox. Next was the ham boiler, a two-story affair of thick tin, but seldom used. Beyond the large open fireplace, again with an individual firebox, was the Rumford oven, always in great demand just before Christmas and Thanksgiving. Made of iron set deep in the brickwork, its door opened by a brass handle while two small ventilators below and above led to the chimney flue that regulated the temperature. When the door was thrown open, a cavern some three feet deep was disclosed with a slatted iron shelf in the middle. In it, the daily bread or delectable cake, the "Molly Saunders" gingerbread and a full dozen pies could be baked at one time.

Beyond the oven was the closet for the family of pots and kettles of iron, brass and copper scoured fresh and bright, with curious skillets, spiders, frying pans and the long-handled bread toaster hinged at the junction of the handle and rack so that the slices of toast could be turned without reaching in where the fire was too hot. The kitchen had a more distant closet where larger things were kept. Roomy store closets, for groceries and the usual kitchen supplies, were often referred to as the pantry. The tongs, poker and fire shovel were always standing near the fireplace in an angle of the brickwork. The turkey wings, saved the sweep of the hearth, hung on the oven knobs. The bunch of iron meat skewers were swinging from a nail and on the soapstone frame of the ham boiler was kept the friendly bellows, always ready to help put new life into a pile of dying embers.

With the elaborate baking and broiling of good things, it is a wonder that the day before Christmas was the special day for the entire family. It was the custom to weigh out and measure the flour, sugar, tea, potatoes and butter, and with ham, turkey, chicken and legs of mutton to pack tempting baskets for families less fortunate for their holiday celebration. It was a busy day and the kitchen was certainly the center of activity. Bundles and cloth bags were stuffed with good things.

These wholesale preparations for feasting were only undertaken prior to a dinner party, so it is not strange that the New Hampshire Feast Day brings to mind not the ordering of a few baskets of fruit by telephone, but a cozy twilight room assembled with heavy, curious implements, reeking with good aromas, noisy with cheerful neighbors and family. In closing, let us not overlook the fact that the kitchen was the place of central heat, a place for the drying of winter mittens, boots and outer clothing and a special gathering place for family and friends.

Now that we have become acquainted with the function and equipment for the operation of the early kitchen, let us spend an afternoon with Polly Ayre as she convinces us that cooking in a fireplace was not the awesome chore that we had always imagined when looking at the spits and jacks, braziers and trivets that surrounded so many early fireplaces, as described earlier.

## A Winter Breakfast on the Farm

As I remember it, a weekend on the farm was an awesome experience, especially the business of breakfast—country style. This is not the run-and-rush meal to which some of us are accustomed. For the farm people it is a businesslike procedure of refueling for the morning's exertion. For the animals it is a sort of roll call and inspection combined with the sociability of boss and employees in a coffee break. The time consumed by the meal in the dining room is insignificant when compared with that necessary for the animals' breakfast, for they have "room service." The amount of walking involved in transferring food from a base of supplies to their individual stomachs is astonishing.

The chores begin early when night is still complete and undisturbed. Of all the busy moments of a farm day, none is more crucial than the one that comes at five in the morning. Once the foot hits the icy bedroom air, there is no turning back; you are committed and the day has begun.

Harry, the man of the house, has made the working arrangements with the fire in the kitchen range, while Polly, his wife, is on her knees before the coal stove in the dining area. The kettle of hot water, their link with yesterday, is removed from the coal stove to its accustomed place on the range, and soon coffee, cereal and bacon are lending a cheerful fragrance to the once cold kitchen. At about this time Harry scratches a hole in the frost on the back windowpane to peer, flashlight in hand, at the thermometer, and announces "ten below."

Breakfast over, the moment inexorably approaches when they must don their outer clothing and start on the "room service" meal.

Animals don't seem to mind being awakened. As Polly passes through the woodshed to the connected barn, her footsteps rouse the family dog, Champ. He opens his eyes, blinks, slowly gets to a standing position, shakes and follows her to the day's business.

Upon arrival, she lifts the covers of the cows' cribs. It is a signal for them to stumble awkwardly to their feet. They don't yawn, but at the first sign of breakfast they are ready to eat the grain that is thrust under their tossing heads.

Next, Polly and Champ proceed to the stable. At the fifth stanchion there is no cow, but a rug of eight cats lying peacefully together in a furry pile, each body fitting into the contours of others so that it seems like one circular mass of cat. As soon as one moves a muscle, another is thrown off balance and the circle is immediately disentangled. The cats right themselves, arch backs, stretch hindquarters, walk away a few feet, sit down and watch until it is certain the disturbance is permanent rather than temporary. Shortly thereafter, three of them reassemble in the nearby basket.

The barn is comfortably warm, though heated by nothing but the energy generated by the great bodies of the animals. The next task of getting down the hay and oats thrusts Polly into a different environment. She ascends the stairs, across a haymow, up a ladder to the very top floor of the barn and crosses the rattling floorboards to the gable end of the barn. Here, under the icy roof boards—polka-dotted with frosted nail heads, where the pitchfork handle seems to turn to solid ice in her hands, where not even so sheer a thing as a cobweb escapes its coating of frost—from this frigid corner she tosses down to the herd below the nutriment stowed away during July's sunshine for just such a time as this.

When these animals have had their fill of hay, it is time for the hens. Carrying the pail of drinking water and accompanied by Champ, Polly receives a royal welcome at the hen house.

Now, the walk to the pigpen takes her by the silo, past the stonewall and down through the garden by a well-trod path. In winter, when the snow crust is slippery or the path is icy, one starts out hopefully, carrying the heavy pail of scalded meal, which was carefully thinned with skimmed milk and flavored with cooked small potatoes; one slip and it's all over.

Upon arrival, the singular pig rises immediately from her bed of straw with a good morning grunt. One thing about this particular pig is that she never questions the suitability of the menu, or the time that breakfast is being served. All she requires is that it is served quickly without bothering about the condition in which she left her supper trough. This arduous task of delivering her breakfast to her room is sometimes rewarded with "tips" of a sort.

Day arrives at the treetops on the hill while twilight still lingers low near the stone wall. The sun's soft rays touch the neat gray waistcoat of a woodpecker upon the walnut tree as he taps for bugs. In a late November dawn, the frost decorations are worth coming out to see. Each weed top, blade of grass, stone and even grains of soil are grown in silver beads. When the sun touches them, they contain a moment of diamond-clad beauty. The common chickweed under the apple tree, each frozen leaf adorned by an unnaturally bright green and coated with the finest traces of frost, has become designed for Christmas wrappings.

The task of serving breakfast is basic to the farm business and is gladly accomplished regardless of the weather.

## Fireplace Cooking with Polly Ayre

Welcome to Polly's kitchen. She is a firm believer that anyone has the ability to cook, that "hidden gift" just waiting to emerge. Sitting at the window with the sun on my back, watching her build up a fire in a matter of minutes, I began to believe her.

She began with crumbled newspaper placed directly on the hearth, added a few dry twigs, leaves and corncobs and placed two good dry logs, one in front and one in back of the kindling. As soon as the fire was burning well, another log, partially green, was placed in front so as to control the draft. "The trick," Polly says, "is not to build the fire too high, well before you are ready to cook so that you will have a good bed of coals. As the fire burns down, add more wood." She reminded me that controlling the heat for cooking is just a matter of careful watching and practice. "Eventually," she continues, "you will know instinctively just how close your pot must be to the fire for proper cooking. Remember, however, that the best wood for fuel in everybody's opinion is hickory. The white and black oaks would be my second choice."

Polly insists that once you have the knack and the basic equipment, anything can be cooked in the fireplace. An iron pot of appropriate size to prepare a meal makes a good beginning to a collection of fireplace cookware. With it you can produce savory soup and stew, a delicious New England boiled dinner or pot pie. An iron pot simmering over the fire served the early eighteenth-century settlers quite well.

A crane is invaluable for adjusting cooking temperatures and swinging a simmering kettle out to remove it from the fire. The earliest homes lacked such luxury, so they made do with lug poles—green logs—installed crosswise in the throat of the chimney, about six feet above the hearth. "It is possible," Polly advises, "to simmer a pot on a high trivet placed over hot coals, although it will take more watching to keep it from burning on the bottom."

"A Dutch oven or bake kettle, footed like the standard pot, but not so tall, with a tight-fitting lid, makes fine breads, cakes and custards. For frying and making pancakes or pone bread, add a large skillet—an old one with legs and a long handle when possible—otherwise a standard iron skillet and a fairly tall trivet may be used."

"If you are going to cook bread in the open fire, sweep a clean spot on the hearth and place a piece of dough directly on the hot bricks. Cover it with an upside-down pot of iron or earthenware, and then cover the pot with embers and pile hot coals around it. Experience will dictate the baking time needed."

These are Polly's "basics," but the possibilities for collecting and using fireplace cooking utensils are limitless: several types of toasters, from long handled forks with two or three tines to footed toasters that accommodate several slices of bread at once; stationary or whirling gridirons for grilling meat; tin kitchens equipped with spits; salamanders (thin plates of iron on long handles) for browning the tops of dishes; trammels, pot hangers and roasting jacks; even waffle wrought irons.

The old hand-wrought kettles and skillets that Polly uses have a patina, but Polly admits, "cast-iron implements from later periods, even new ones, can be given a cooking surface that is just as good." She advises, however, "When you acquire a piece of ironware, new or old, it should be washed with hot, soapy water, rinsed well, dried thoroughly and rubbed with a little cooking oil or fresh lard to prevent rust. After oiling, a new pan should be placed in a warm oven, about two hundred degrees, for a few hours to season. Even badly rusted ironware can be returned to usefulness."

Her method of restoring old iron is very simple. "After scouring off the surface rust with steel wool or sand, keep the piece out where you can see it, and each time you wash dishes, wash the pot, dry it thoroughly, rub it with fresh lard and heat it by the fire—an hour or two, or however long the fire lasts. A few weeks of this treatment and the piece will acquire a smooth surface that makes it stick-proof. If the piece has been painted, the paint is removed with a commercial solvent, steel wool and a mountain of rags and then given the wash-oil-heat treatment."

"The real pleasure of fireplace cooking," Polly admits, "comes from putting the early utensils to work over the open hearth and letting the 'hidden gift' take over to turn out a warm and satisfying meal."

Below are some recommended dishes:

### Dutch Oven Corn Bread

¼ cup melted butter
1 tablespoon sugar
1 teaspoon salt
3 teaspoons baking powder

1 cup cornmeal (roasted and stone-ground if possible)
2 eggs
1½ cups milk
2 cups flour

Melt butter. Combine dry ingredients in a large bowl. Beat eggs and milk together and pour over dry ingredients. Stir until smooth. Add melted butter and stir until well mixed. Pour into a buttered Dutch oven—the batter should not be more than 1½ inches deep—and cover. Place the Dutch oven at the edge of the fire and a few coals around it and shovel other coals on the lid. It should bake in about 25 to 30 minutes, depending on the fire. It is wise to check it after approximately 20 minutes; it is done when a straw or sharp knife thrust into the center comes out clear.

### Chicken Pot Pie

3–4 pound stewing chicken
salt, pepper and a pinch of saffron
4 or 5 potatoes, peeled and cut in half
2 eggs
2 tablespoons cooking oil
2 cups flour

Cut the stewing chicken into pieces. Place in a 5- or 6-quart kettle and cover with water. Add salt, pepper and a pinch of saffron. Boil gently until the chicken is tender and can be removed from the bone easily. Remove chicken and take the meat from the bone and cut into small pieces. Return meat to the broth. Add potatoes and bring to a hard boil.

While the potatoes are cooking, mix eggs, oil and flour together, adding water a spoonful at a time until dough can be rolled about ⅛ of an inch thick. Cut into 2-inch squares and drop one at a time into boiling broth so they do not stick together. Boil 30 to 40 minutes or until they are tender. Serve—very hot—in soup bowls.

### White Bread

Take ¾ of a peck of fine flower and salt in as much as will season it, then heat as much milk as will season it lukewarm. Hold it high when you pour it on to make it light, and mingle with your milk 4 or 5 spoonfuls of good yeast. Work your paste well and then let it lie rising by the fire. Your oven will be heated in an hour and a half, then shut it up a quarter of an hour, in which space make up your loaves and then set them in the oven. An hour and a half will bake them.

## The Old Parlor Stove

How distressing it must have been to the one-horse New Hampshire farmer when the old-time parlor heater joined the buffalo robes, soapstones and long underwear in humanity's junk heap of outmoded accoutrements. The old heater was such a magnificent centerpiece. One of the epochal events on the homestead was when grandfather said, "Mary, I guess we can afford the new parlor stove you have been wanting."

The mail-order catalogue's description was satisfyingly forthright. The Acme Brilliant Base Burner, according to the catalogue, was "the finest the world produces; a dream of an artist in design and trimming. The equal of any baseburner made by any maker. It embodies all the very latest, handsomest and best features of every other high grade burner."

There was nickel embellishment work all over the stove. There was a handsome nickel-plated urn on top, a heavy, nickel-plated swing top, nickel corner wings, nickel hearth plate and ash door panel. The burner stood on a heavy, nickel-plated frame with stocky nickel legs. It was about five feet high and weighed about three hundred pounds.

These old stoves represented something pivotal in man's climb to what one hesitatingly calls higher civilization. More than two centuries ago, Lady Mary Montague wrote from the continent to her sister in England concerning the porcelain stoves. "They have brought these stoves to perfection. They lengthen their summer as they please...They are so far from spoiling the form of a room that they add very much to the magnificence of it."

There are many old-timers today who push a little metal lever on a wall for more heat, but still remember the parlor heaters. It was a lad's task—around 1930—to keep the wood box filled with solid chunks of knotty maple, oak and old apple wood.

Around the stove the young people did their homework, while Mother worked at the never-ending mending and darning and answering questions on how to spell "Winnipesaukee," and what was the capital of

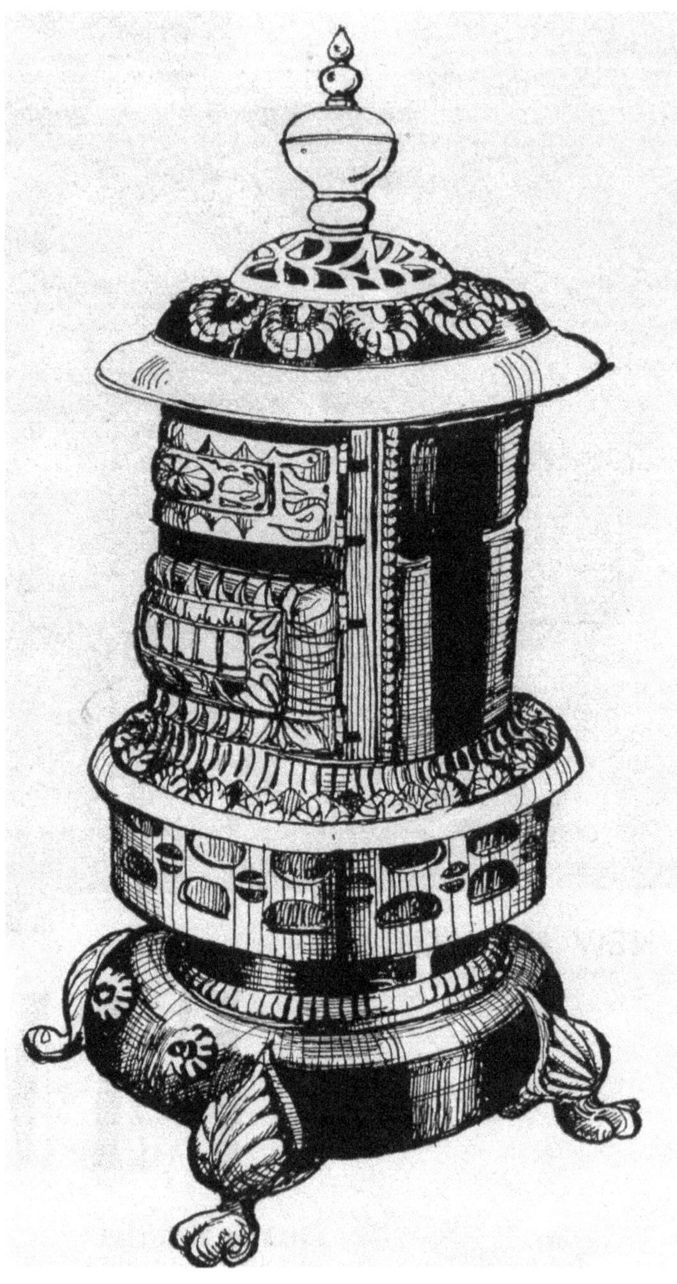

In the warmth of the farm living room, the parlor heater represented home and family. It stood for something solid and meaningful in our country tradition. *Drawing by Jean Price Horne.*

Massachusetts. Father sat in his old Morris chair, reading the Almanac or looking over the newest issue of the *New Hampshire Farm Journal.* These stoves did not replace the kitchen fireplace, but were an added convenience to the parlor heat.

During one of those cold, wintry evenings, the whole family joined in making out the spring mail-order list or discussing the new varieties of plant seeds to order from the seed catalogue. Around the parlor heater, boys and girls played flinch, authors and checkers when home lessons were done.

In the morning, the youngest member of the family would grab his clothes in his bedroom and quickly hustle downstairs to dress in front of the warmth of the parlor stove.

Through the isinglass door of the tall gleaming stove, the red and orange flames painted ever-changing pictures. And as the burning chunks crackled and sang and the pictures flashed and faded and flashed again, a lad would look up from his book and dream of a world waiting—a world of excitement and challenge far from the homestead. Now a man looks into the leaping flames of a fireplace and knows that the world of adventure is still waiting. The nickel-plated heater had always fostered dreams, which had given meaning to many lives. Even though the stove has vanished, its fond memories still linger on in the minds of many.

## The Upland Pastures

Our New Hampshire farms were self-sufficient, for the early settlers had little opportunity to market for supplies away from their own farms. Their land and homes had to be shrewdly organized with meadowland for hay, fields for grain, a wood lot and an upland pasture. Each section fit into their economic scheme. In the following narrative, we will examine the importance of the pasture to the whole farm complex.

The upland pasture was most important, for it furnished feed for the cattle from the middle of May until frost. The upland pasture was most often studded with weather-grayed boulders and lichen-covered ledge outcroppings. Sprawling green patches of juniper bushes formed an irregular pattern on the hillside. There were clumps of gray birches. Inevitably, in one corner of the pasture, there would be a continuous spring bubbling from the ground that would flow into the moss-covered wooden trough. There was always an area of high-bush berries, which meant juicy pies in early autumn and jars of the blue-black fruit for the cellar cupboard.

Let us pause for a moment, for we should not pass without mentioning the abundance of wild blueberries in New Hampshire. About the only regular care given most blueberry fields is burning them over every two or three years. This serves to prune the bushes, which stimulates new growth and induces a heavy crop of fruit. If the plants are not burned, they soon become crowded and spindling and their yield is drastically reduced. Burning is done in early spring, when the soil is wet or even frozen, so that the roots and the mat of organic matter they grow in are not damaged.

Blueberries are harvested by hand with metal scoop-rakes, something like those used for cranberries. The fields are marked off into straight lanes with string so that they may be picked over systematically. This also discourages pickers from skipping the plants that have fewer berries. The fruit is run through a winnowing machine to remove bits of stems and leaves and then packed into baskets or crates, all without being touched by human hands. A large portion of the crop is canned; some of it is frozen and a little is sold as fresh fruit.

Throughout the pasture, masses of pink roses, forming bright clumps of color against gray rocks and sun, tanned the sun-glazed grasses. Spotted clumps of sheep laurel held their stiff spikes, and when goldenrod time came, coveys of the yellow blooms burst forth along the stonewall fences. Over the walls the alders would lean, pasture pine and scrub oaks. Beneath the wall was the home of the philosophical, bewhiskered chipmunk that always seemed to get to his den a few yards ahead of the farm collie. In the highest corner was the maple grove with its dilapidated sugarhouse. The shade of the trees was always a welcome to the stock on the hot August days and a place of warmth in late September.

Our first settlers quickly found that the upland pasture wasn't the best for plowing and harrowing, for it was steep and filled with granite rocks, but it would serve its purpose for a long time as ample grazing for the family cattle.

Periodically, the grass of the upland fields and low-lying meadows had to be cut. Machinery was not available, so the country farmer depended on his skill with the scythe—his tool of the trade. Even today some of us can remember when a dozen men, one offset behind the other, cut their swaths across big fields in the early morning when dew was still on the grass.

Mowing by hand was considered an art. Those who had mastered the rhythmic precision of the process had an instinctive sense of timing and balance. The mower was as particular about his scythe as the artist about his fine-gauge instrument. The tool must feel right to the hands; the balance must suit, and the weight had to match the man's strength. A good farmer insisted that his scythe was made of the best steel and could take a fine edge.

To watch a master mower in action was to watch poetry in motion. Bent forward from his hip, he swung with ease and calculated strokes. With the heel of the tool close to the ground, he laid windows of sweet-scented grasses in paralleled rows. With feet a few inches apart, he would edge forward with steady, short steps. At intervals he would pause, rest the end of the scythe on the turf, pull a whetstone from the long, narrow pocket on the leg of his overalls and renew the edge of the blade. With sure, long strokes, the stone rang against the steel; then with his thumb, the mower tested the renewed cutting edge.

A day or two before his haying got underway, the farmer would trim out from around his outbuildings, around his garden and along the stone walls and fences.

It isn't mowing by hand, as the farmers of yesterday knew it, but the countryman still enjoyed the feel of his balanced outfit as the razor sharp blade swished through the pasture grass and clover.

Time to harvest is not far off. There was a sense of urgency in the regular haying season, for during those hot July days the farm family stretched every sinew to get the crop under cover as quickly as possible. When mowing time came there was a different spirit about the land. The rush of the season's work was past and the main crops were due.

The countryman prized his past cutting of clover and timothy as the hay for his best cows or for his favorite horse.

Most likely, light frosts had laid on it, but we also knew the touch of early fall rains after the dryness and the heat of August. The farmer went at the cutting leisurely. The short grass had a nostril-tingling fragrance. During the mellow September sun, it cured very quickly and the aroma of sweet, drying hay filled the air. It was easy to mow due to its short length. In the same field, where the horses leaned hard against their collars for the main cutting, they pulled the singing-mowing machine at a brisk, easy clip.

The view is Mount Starr King, from Whitefield, New Hampshire, 1910. The pasture had a surprising amount of grazing grass. Among the boulders and between patches of junipers, the farm stock would easily find the sparse, sweet grass.

On many of the hill farms, mowing time was when mother and the girls of the family enjoyed tramping the loads in the hayrack. As for the farmer, he wasn't so particular about building a big load; an extra trip meant little when there was but a small harvest and time wasn't pressing.

On the quiet, brooding days, when the sun's rays soaked into brown stubble and the early September haze laid over the upland pastures and mountain slopes, mowing time was a good period of the farmer's calendar. It was the last crop from the hayfield. Mowing time meant the end of his harvest season. When this crop was safely under cover, the early farmer was ready for the frost bound months ahead.

## MEMORIES OF THE OLD BARN

For many years I have wanted to return to the old homestead; one day last winter I did just that. I remember the old dirt road, but it wasn't the old road that was important—it was the places on the road that had changed. The Burrows barn was no longer there, the apple orchard had disappeared and the back pasture had all grown up.

The old place wasn't the same either. There was no smoke coming out of the chimney, and no dog in the yard barking me a welcome. There was no one there, and all was quiet—abandoned. The old apple tree in the back was no longer there. How those apples used to put my teeth on edge! The field had grown up, and I wondered if there were any woodchucks left. How the family dog did like to shake them up!

The farm was filled with magic then. The back pond was blue, thick with early ice, and drifts of snow made saucers around the clothesline posts. The big lake below the field sparkled and snapped with frozen stress marks etching it like the furrows under the eyes of Uncle Al.

I went down to the barn. It was the same except there were paper shingles on the roof instead of wood. The barn door was closed, but someone had forgotten to lock it. I had a hard time opening it; the back pulley was off the track.

I cautiously went in. The place was empty. It should have been full of hay that time of year. How I longed for the hay smell and the cow smell with a little bit of horse aroma mixed in.

Father sorted the hay; there was always a year's supply ahead. New hay made them sweat too much. The clover, June grass and oats were put on the scaffolds. The mixed hay was put in the big bays. Father liked a little meadow hay to feed in March—said it was a tonic for the cows after eating the other hay all winter.

This was a child's country playroom. It was great fun to climb up on the high beams and jump off into the hay. Sometimes we'd jump down into the hay clean up to our shoulders. If it wasn't too far down to the hay, we tried a couple of flips. I had more than one lame neck doing it.

The horse stalls were all on the right just as you entered through the door. The stalls were there so if the barn caught on fire, we could get the horses out of the barn quickly. They were all closed in, with a sliding door in back of them that you closed on winter nights to keep out the cold. The stalls were all gray stanchion and undulating brown and spotted white. Soft eyes under wrinkled lids, slack chewing jaws, animal habitation, but room for a small body in red coat and boots with melting snow on them to prowl and cuddle and dream dreams of swift chase on green hills that had been ages back, before the snow came.

I opened one of the doors and looked in. I used to play in there a lot. Jerry did not like anyone on his back, but Nellie was different. For two or three apples you could sit on her back and ride with King Arthur, or for half a dozen carrots you could chase Indians if you didn't holler too loud.

I went in. It was clean enough even though there were some cow buns here and there, but it was damp and clammy. It used to be nice and warm in the winter. How good it was to go in there when you came to do the chores! Old Bessy always talked through her nose to me when I went in. If I found any sweet grass when I pitched down the hay, I saved it just for her. After she had eaten it, the sweet fragrance was noticeable on her breath.

In late fall the barn floor was filled with corn shucks and cartloads of pumpkins. The cows and I played ninepins with them. The cows didn't really play, but they ate up the busted ones.

The corn was husked on rainy days. A neighbor and his family would come over on an evening now and then, and we would husk for a couple of hours. If Father knew they were coming, he would get a jug of sweet cider from the barn; the womenfolk never husked.

What a good time we had husking! We hunted woodchucks and hedgehogs, talked about the schoolteacher, and if there was a new girl on the school we talked about her, too.

The womenfolks always brought something, and after we finished we went up to the house and had a party. There was apple pie and chocolate cake. Occasionally mother would put a dish of aged McIntosh apples on the table just to tease us kids. She always took them off after a while and put on a dish of fresh fruit.

There was a certain beam on the south side of the barn that had a knothole just big enough to reach into. I kept my special things in there. There were some things a boy wasn't supposed to have.

When that old family cat would come around, I would go there and take out a tin tube about a foot long. I would put a bean in the end, take a long breath of air and blow hard. That old cat always went racing home.

Sometimes in the summer when it was hot, my big sister would act mean and ugly to me. When she was that way I would get some tissue paper and cut it into little squares, take cornmeal out of the grain chest and make some torpedoes like the ones we had on the Forth of July. Then I would go to that knothole and get my slingshot. Some of those torpedoes shot into her bedroom window most always fixed her.

The barn activity building at Geneva Point Camp, Moultonboro, New Hampshire, 1943.

Kids were not allowed to have tobacco. It took a lot of trading and bickering to get some. I gave ten cents, an old jackknife and a fishing pole. It was a big plug with a metal tag on it. There was a picture of a dog on the tag, and the words "Old Honesty."

When my friend Stu came to see me and we played grown-ups, I got my plug out of the knothole. We put some in our mouths and chewed and spit, and swaggered around and talked big. We were really grown up. Mother smelled some on my breath one time and washed my mouth out with yellow soap. After that I always went to the barnyard and washed my mouth out at the watering tub.

I had a hard time closing the barn door. I wanted it closed tight. There were a lot of memories in that barn and I wanted them to stay there.

## The Winter Woodpile

Fred and Ralph were a couple of die-hards when it came to sawing wood. Not that they had anything against the chainsaw, which could mess up enough wood in a day to last you a year. They both admit the chainsaw to be a great invention and a boon to loggers, but Fred and Ralph liked sawing wood by hand, the way people like to fish or hunt. You see, they like to talk while sawing, but with a chainsaw you can't hear your own voice, let alone the other fellow's.

Shuttling rhythmically between them, their saw seemed to hum a drowsy, rocking lullaby, and all of nature murmured with the action of each stroke. All about them the air teemed with myriad insects mesmerized by the warm, yellow sunlight. The foliage passed in season with the strands of dark-green spruces among the riotous maple colors, suggesting the presence within a dreamlike palace.

"Best time of year to saw your wood." Fred's nasal New Hampshire twang blended with the thrumming of the saw. "Fell your trees and climb 'em while the sap's still in the leaves. Then the logs saw better and your wood dried faster."

If it hadn't been for sawing wood by hand, they wouldn't have gotten to know one another as well as they did. For years Fred had helped Ralph saw the winter wood. True, Fred got paid and boarded—he was the boss, the officiated high priest of those autumnal rites. Fred and Ralph made music, with the crosscut saw as their own instrument, aided by a few saw-wedges, a couple of axes, a light sledge and two flat files. Ralph informed me that yellow birch sawed easier than maple and the unimpeded saw took greedy bites out of the less resistant wood. "There's an easy, effortless swing to the arm, but the sawing lacks the fine-grained, cleaner cut of maple. Still the sawyer's enjoyment was not diminished, for yellow birch is not gushy like balsam, which stifles the saw with pulpy, excelsior-like sawdust and waxes it with its gummy bark."

On the shady side of seventy, Fred seemed ageless, and sawing wood wouldn't hurt. Somewhere between fifty and sixty he got cast into a mold that retained its form and hardness. He lived alone, raising potatoes, beans and pumpkins, sugaring a little, berrying in season, water witching for summer folk, limin' bees in the fall and sawing wood.

That was when Ralph began to take notice. To Ralph he was much like a piece of the White Mountain scenery, a pokeweed on the Tamworth landscape. But as they sawed wood season after season, Fred took on stature. Grain by grain his character sifted out, until there it was, a meaningful little pile, like the sawdust from a knot in the wood.

Again the easy rhythm of the saw was suddenly lost to us. The saw's teeth grated, the blade itself trembled. The sawdust no longer flowed out but spit out in separate motes. Fred inserted a wedge in the crack.

Still the saw dragged on the arm and whined like a pup. It wasn't the labor they minded; it was the knot's insinuation into the rhythm of the muscles, into the saw's respiration. But the two kept at it, and within a minute or two they cut through the knot and the saw again breezed hungrily. Its teeth ground out the hardness of the wood and spilled it in foamy cataracts.

With his country-wise counsel, Fred had saved Ralph no end of trouble. Ralph would ask for his advice. Much like the New Hampshire native, unless you ask, he would let you make a fool of yourself and say nothing. He would let you dig a spring line up a rocky hillside to a spring he knew would run out the first dry spell. When Ralph asked him why he didn't warn him, he would reply, "You didn't ask me."

Even when he asked, Fred would always presume not to instruct him. "If it were mine, I'd do thus and so." Possibly he would have directed his attention to the ways of nature, as to when or whether he should seed his lawn in the fall or in the spring. Fred would think for a moment and then answer, "Well, now, when does the good Lord do his seedin?"

"In the fall, isn't it?"

"Well, He ain't no fool."

Fred lived the old life, a life of absolute self-reliance and self-dependence. His chores, his heating and cooking arrangements, his water supply—the entire pattern of his life, or any part of it—could not have been disrupted by a dead spark plug, a dead battery, blown-out fuses or transformers or condensers, frozen pipes, the tyranny of dripping faucets or the erratic flushing toilets, or the whims of plumbers, mechanics or electricians. Fred had never surrendered reliance of his own ingenuity and ability to handle matters in his own individualistic way.

Fred wasted nothing, least of all the movements of his body. He was sparing with his gestures, sparing with the twitching of his face muscles. When he laughed, only his throat laughed. His face and eyes never smiled. The strokes of his axe were always clean and precise, the bit striking where it's meant to. He drew the saw in his direction just so much and no more, and then released it to his partner, Ralph.

Each succeeding morning, as they neared the end of the wood sawing, the air would get cold. The frosty grass crackled underfoot, and the insects would be benumbed. But as the sun rose from behind the spruce-crested ridge and threw its diaphanous mantle about them, they could hear the rustle of the earth as it stirred from its shallow lethargy.

Let it come. The huge pile of bucked-up hardwood drying in the sun was a comforting sight. There was reassurance in every block. When you see wood year after year, the way Fred and Ralph did, and burn it to cook with and warm your homestead, you become familiar with the temperaments, characteristics and qualities of different woods. You come to know them by grain and bark, degree of hardness, the way they burn and saw and split and the scents they give forth as they burned. You come to feel about woods as you do about people, and you treat them accordingly. You do not have the respect for the hard-splitting, quick-burning, yellow birch that you have for the clean-splitting, longer-lasting maple. As for beech, it is good, clean wood, saws well, splits neatly and burns brightly when dry. But there's something prosaic about beech. It lacks the high nobility of maple and oak, or the impulsiveness of yellow birch.

"Well," announced Fred as the last block toppled off, "you've got wood enough to burn." He would take a long, slow pull on his old pipe and blow a cloud of smoke into the brisk autumn air. The smoke smelled more like sawdust than tobacco—that would be Fred.

Unlike Fred and Ralph's use of the saw, it was the axe that had hewn history in New Hampshire. There's more choppin' wood than just cutting down a tree. There is a certain nostalgia and romance in using an axe, rifle and hoe.

When a man goes into the wood lot on a winter's day, he feels a kinship with the calm of nature. Here among the trees that had seen the miracle of spring, the fruition harvest and the blizzards of winter for better than a century, the ills and cares that infest man and his society fall into proper perspective. The pine, hemlock and fir murmur among themselves. Beeches, maples and oak are traced against the winter sky like dry point etchings. Birds sing their song, the chipmunks dash from bush to bush and the partridge whir up with startling suddenness.

The country gentleman would chop wood and now saw it. He would select his tree with care, and would enjoy swinging the sharp-bladed axe. Thick chips would fly and the pleasant, pungent aroma of fresh wood would scent the clear air. But when day was over, he would walk down the pasture slope toward the lights in the farmhouse. A man who had been chopping knew that he had increased his wealth by more than a pile of logs in the wood lot. This was a time when it was an axiom of the countryside that you could judge a farmer by his woodpile. The good

The winter woodpile located in the upper pasture.

farmer took pride in his fuel supply. In the winter or the early spring, it was sawed, split and stacked in the woodshed.

On frosty evenings, when cold air hung like a blanket over the hills and valleys, many farmers paused as they came to the barn. The yellow light of the lantern made a picture as it played over the stacked tiers.

A real country woodshed was a place of deep, fundamental satisfaction. It represented honest labor—the cutting in the wood lot, the trimming and hauling, the sawing as the whirring knife-edged teeth sang through the logs and the splitting as the axe flashed down and struck the exact spot so that a chunk separated along the grain, the stacking as the symmetrical tiers rose toward the woodshed attic floor.

A woodshed that had been used for years had a tangy aroma. There's the resinous zip of the pine limbs, the acridness of red oak, the zesty tang of old apple wood, the bland smoothness of the sugar maple and beech, the peculiarly pungent odor of hemlock and the clear exhilarating smell of cedar.

This is part of our heritage and legacy, the same as johnnycake, pancake and maple syrup.

The woodshed connected to the main house. *Drawing by Bruce D. Heald, 1989.*

'89

## A Country Boy Remembers

Were you fortunate to have been born and raised in the country, and did you have to drive the cows to pasture? If so, then you can remember getting up at five every summer morning and starting each day by turning your own cow loose. You leisurely made your way down through the village, picking up some recruits until you entered the pasture lane with better than half a dozen head. It was a little more than a mile to the pasture, and you made that trip twice a day—but what's a few miles for a boy of twelve?

The season usually began in May and lasted until heavy frost killed the grass. You got two dollars a head for driving those cows, which meant that at the end of the summer you probably received twenty-four dollars, which your father promptly took and deposited into your savings account. You did not drive cows for money; it was just part of being a farm boy. Now, to be sure, you acquired valuable folklore that was to sweeten your days to the end of your life, but at that time you were not conscious of that.

Please allow me to reminisce with you of those early boyhood days on the farm. It was the first day in May. How cold it was! The day sparkled like diamonds on the grass. How it made my bare feet ache! How good it was when I struck a patch of warm sand in the road. Spring was in my blood, and how happily I moved about whistling and yelling for joy. So did my cow. She was a dark red Durham—about as long as a boxcar. The minute she came out into the sun, she stood on her head and made a wild kick at the weathervane on top of the barn. Oh, do I remember how she raced down the road and was determined to take the wrong turn. When I found I could not keep it up much longer, I grabbed her nose and pulled her hard around, and fourteen hundred pounds of cow shot into the air and came down squarely on her back. Well, I was some surprised to realize that a hundred pounds of boy could flop a half-ton of cow like that. I thought that I had killed her, but was relieved to find that I only slowed her enthusiasm so that she was willing to follow the right road.

I learned the hard way what mean dispositions cows have—how they will always take the wrong road when the right one is easier or how they will jump out of the pasture to feed. My cow always seemed to get home in the morning before I did, and then I had to drive her back to the pasture again. I promptly resolved to stop that, so I tied her head down to her foot, and when I turned her into the field that morning, she slipped off a tussock and rolled down the bank into the nearby brook. I was sure scared. I thought for sure that I had broken her neck. Instead, she broke the rope and was in the village, grazing on the open green when I got back home.

I can't help but remember that narrow escape I had when the herd got over the wall into the enclosure about the slaughter barn. I sat on a post and laughed to witness them pitch dirt over their backs and walk stiff-legged. But time was passing, so I gradually trotted over to drive them out. I only had time to say "Whay!" once, when Widow Burrow's cow, who ordinarily hadn't brains enough to last her overnight, put her head down and came after me like a wildcat. I passed my own shadow on the way to the fence, but even at that I was not quick enough, and widow Burrow's animal put a horn through the seat of my pants and promptly helped me in my flight out of the enclosure.

A cow is a slow-moving animal, but she can kick quicker than lightning. I sure learned this on that morning when, in sweeping out the barn, I accidentally tickled her hock with a broom. I suddenly found myself sitting on a haycock halfway across the barn. The only reason I wasn't killed was because I was so close that she lifted me rather than striking me.

I remember the mornings I got a ride back from the village. Often I would watch for one of the village boys bringing milk to the cheese factory; I always heard him coming long before he appeared. It was all downhill full of stones, of course, and that old buckboard, and the two large cans of booming covers made plenty of noise.

On those trips to the pasture, I learned about birds—and every other living thing. Those Devil's Darning Needles, which hovered over the stagnant pool—best we keep our eyes on them! They sewed up the lips of those who told lies. Oh, I remember how surprised I was to find a person who knew nothing about birds. When I was twelve years old I could identify better than fifty of them. I even knew their songs, and what kind of eggs they laid. That big greenish one, spotted with brown; that was a crow. How about the almost spherical ivory one? Yellow Hammer. The pale, pointed one, laced all over with straggling lines? Baltimore oriole. No sir! Nobody could fool me with birds' eggs. Thank God for that boyish folklore that has made life richer and more worth living.

The gathering of the cows as we prepare to leave the farm.

At night, when school was over and the sun was setting and the long shadows were streaming across the broad meadows, I remember how I padded over the hot, sandy road to the pasture and found the cows with dripping udders just waiting for me at the bars. I remember how carefully we brought them home, not to run, for that would hurt the milk.

Can you look back upon all these days past? If you can, you will never have a weary hour. Waiting in loneliness, enduring a dull speech, lying sleepless in bed—just close your eyes and reminisce those earlier days, when.

## The Old Mountain Roads

More times than not, we're in so much of a hurry to get from one place to another that Interstate 93 seems like a blessing. But, in a frantic urge to be somewhere else on time, we can't help but notice the boredom of these new highways; they lack something. The old country road—with trees close to its edge, shady and quiet, with now and then a covered bridge over a mountain stream—was the sort of road you could drive on as fast as really necessary or was good for you and yet feel you were then and there at the time in a place that was enjoyable, and you were not just in motion. As useful as country roads can be, the old road that has been abandoned has the most charm of any and takes its place in the heart of anyone who likes to walk beneath the open New Hampshire skies.

There are hundreds of miles of abandoned and less-traveled dirt roads in our state—some because they went through a section where the farms themselves were abandoned. Perhaps newer and wider roads have taken their places. But, whatever the reason, they constitute one of the greatest attractions, not for those who are in a hurry or who wish to tour the state, but for those who wish to slow down and take a walk or leisurely ride on the back abandoned roads.

While walking on an abandoned road, you don't have to watch for oncoming traffic or inhale the exhaust fumes. You don't have to hurry; you're really not going anywhere. Things don't speed by before they have a real chance to register in your mind or memory.

The length of these abandoned roads may go more than a mile from the traveled highway, but it's a good walk—quiet and peaceful. It goes up over a hill in a heavy wooded area. A brook has washed out its roadbed, but you can walk on the side easily. Great archways of maples, oak and pine frame its way. Halfway up the hill is a solitary gravestone of an early settler. It is surrounded by a stone wall marking out one rod square. On top of the hill is a graveyard, abandoned to the woods—its many stones moss-stained, awry and fallen. Nearby are the granite steps to a schoolhouse that isn't there any more. Going farther, you walk on a narrow path cut through alders and then burst out of them with the road lying broad and smooth and straight among tall pines and spruces. Farther on it goes through a grove of birches, any one of which would double the value of a man's residence if it were in his front yard.

On such a road you can take time to reflect and examine the ancient stone culverts, and possibly marvel at the work that went into constructing them. You can recall the history-making incident that took place here, and as on some sections of the old Province Road, which traveled from Laconia to Plymouth, imagine the shades of men with flintlock muskets on their way home from some conflict at Penacook or Boscawen.

Whenever I go down Interstate 93 and look over to Sanbornton and see an old road, it beckons to be explored. The unknown lures me on to see what is just around the bend of one of those roads.

There's something about an abandoned road that speaks of the people who once used it as a modern boulevard. There's something in the walls that run beside it and the grass-grown surface or the stones washed out along its course, in the brooks and streams that cross it and the trees that shade it, in the darkness of the woods on either side, or the smooth sunlit ledges it goes over, that takes you out of the hurried world into a world of its own.

Not all the roads in the backcountry are abandoned. Take, for example, the less-traveled roads in the North Country off the old road near Swift River, which was used primarily by the logging companies. It was seldom repaired in many places, particularly at the steepest parts. All that could be washed away has gone long ago, leaving nothing but ledges of granite and loose worn stones.

The asters are beginning to fringe the way. Goldenrod waves its head. Its small arching boughs, feathered with gold, light the wayside, shine along the fence corners and glow in patches all through the distant field. It follows us up the mountainside, glittering along the edge of the laurel bush, beautifully pictured on the deep green and varnished leaves. A young leaf of the laurel, just come of age, greets its newcomers with innocence.

At the next rise in the road, we come to a stop and take foot on a side path, leaving the vehicle resting by the side of the road.

Little silver-threaded streams are descending the side of the rocks framed with the sweetest variety of vegetation. Such an aroma of pine that with occasional glances at the distant valley below, we are totally engrossed in nature's beauty. In the distance, a waterfall is heard, mellowed to a deep, grand murmur. It took only a moment and there it is, open in full view. It is only a few feet wide and drops a hundred feet or more straight down the mountain's edge. The brisk waters embrace an insensible rock, and quickly dash down beyond in a double fall. It comes together and widens over that shelving rock, rushing headlong into a crystal pool. Then, like a watery hand at the exit, it divides into five fingers, each sparkling with myriads of diamonds. The alacrity with which the separated currents make motion is magnetizing—the whirls,

The lonesome road through the notch in the White Mountains. To the right on the side of the cliff is the Pulpit Rock.

the side quirks, the petty impetuosities, the splitting and uniting, the plunging and emerging—until the distributed waters pool themselves once more, and finally glance back up with a grave and placid face. Farther below are the cascades and pools in which the water whirls around like a kitten running after its tail.

Upon returning to our vehicle, we again ascend the solitude of the mountain road. We wind round the side of the mountain's upper cone, having a deep, gorge-like valley on our left, at the bottom of which roars one of the most spectacular of mountain streams. Once again we take foot and leave our vehicle and follow down this stream until it begins its descent on the east front of the mountain. We enter a gorge. If you enjoy solitude, wilderness and nature's silent beauty, you would certainly find it worth the time and effort to climb through it. Our moments are peaceful. Harmonic sounds engulf the ear and soul; it is a moment to reflect by the side of the old mountain road.

Chapter Three

# Springtime in the Country

When the bugles of spring sound in New Hampshire valleys, they echo in the hearts of its people everywhere. Memories locked as tight as a winter brook stir to life and burst through the mind in a tumult of recollection.

From marshy lands and small ponds at twilight rises the shrill peeping of frogs, that constant, indescribably lonely chorus. More than other sound, this floods the mind with a thousand memories. To walk along some country roads in the gathering dusk, a soft wind in your face and the air filled with that lonely cadence, is to drop the present from your shoulders and stroll into a past that is far away and long ago.

As the season unfolds, the tang of smoke from grass fires yields to the fragrance of apple orchards or bursting buds and opening flowers until the air is heavy with the scent of spring.

With the blossom-laden air coming in the window, I am lulled to sleep by the soft May rain that patters on fresh new leaves and on the shingles of the roof.

At the mossy doorsteps of a thousand forest-captured cellar holes bloom wild roses and purple lilacs, until the air itself is like a benediction to the nature-awakened memory of those who have been, by man, so utterly forgotten.

This view is Mount Washington from Intervale looking northwest from North Conway, New Hampshire, 1940s. Here the plush meadows and pasture land are beginning to blossom in the new spring.

The open country road, lying faintly white and still beneath the stars, lures us on. The crisp, clear, windy air of Northern mountain notches tingles the blood. For through it all runs a longing that grips the mind just as nature seizes the land itself and frees it from the clutch of winter. Spring has swept up the river valleys and across the open lakes and ponds of New Hampshire.

On this particular evening, these waters are flooding the meadows. The air has a damp chill despite the clearness of the atmosphere, and it is interrupted by sudden, spasmodic blasts of wind. The road that runs through the valley is winding and rolling. On the one side comprises the typical riverbed meadowland, decorated with grand elms whose branches sway in rhythm with the spring breeze, and interrupted by the graceful, curving, sandy banks and swift, dark waters of the river.

It was here in this peaceful background that our poet, John Greenleaf Whittier, found such a plentiful store of enjoyment and inspiration. It was here that he loved to watch the shadows play on the meadow grass and creep over the dark pines on the rolling hills. It was here that he loved to see the neighboring peaks of Chocorua, Paugus and Whiteface outlined against the vivid mountain blueness, or wrung into a somber damp and grayness that is the mountain's own. And it was here that he loved to hear the northwest wind as it blew from the notches to play with the slender arms of the elms and torment the river into a multitude of ripples.

This particular night the sunset was of unusual loveliness and gorgeous shades of purple and crimson touched the valley and made the outer world seem for a moment so commonplace. The cold, rushing streams from the mountains have started to answer the call of spring. They flood the valley and make it even more beautiful. The elms and birch are in their acquiescent mood, and their leafless branches ever groping to touch the darkness. The gibbous moon shining above softly touches the pines on the summit, creating a silver fringe against the sky. The moonlight shines clearly over the encircling mountain ranges, creating white, glassy paths on the cold waters, and scattering unearthly, mystical reflections everywhere.

## The Old Swimmin' Hole

During these hot, sticky summer days the sun reluctantly pulls itself above the horizon's brow and begins its course across a washed blue sky. The valley mist blossoms briefly, and quietness prevails in the country air. Each hushed period precedes a time of seasonal activity. These are times of muted music when quietness rests thickly on the countryside. Golden pollen drifts from the corn tassels to the green skeins of drooping sod beneath and the tall elms in the meadow stand motionless.

Occasionally, a song sparrow takes position on the garden gate and renders a song to break this natural stillness of the valley.

In the distance is heard the muffled feet of our country boy who has finished his chores and is en route to the old swimmin' hole at the Pemigewasset River in West Campton. Hidden quietly by willows, this sanctuary is where the young men can swim, dive and splash without encumbering raiment.

To the discriminating youth, a swimmin' hole, unlike a public town beach, must have a number of essential accessories in addition to its seclusion. It must have a deep spot where a long, overhanging plank

The Pemigewasset River and valley looking north to the Franconia Mountains from West Campton in the White Mountains.

gives him a chance for a high flip for his dive. It most certainly must have a sandbar where he may rest between dives. As an added attraction, the perfect spot is where there is an overhanging bank where the water fowl and water snakes retreat when not invaded by the swimmers.

The best time of day for this activity was usually about four in the afternoon. The monotonous drudgery of labor is over and Father says, "Well, I guess we'll call it a day. You get your swim and then bring the cows home." There's a race to the river and a flinging aside of the overalls, shirt, shoes and socks. There are few pleasures more enjoyable than the first plunge into cold water on a hot midsummer day.

## BROOK FISHING

If we could turn back the clock, the banks on any mountain river and stream would be crowded with small boys and their dogs. Of all the days of our youth, the most delightful were those we spent with a fishhook and a can of worms by the brook that skirted the farm.

Weekdays were taken up with school and chores, but Saturday was our own and from early spring until late fall we haunted the banks. There was a can of worms under the back porch, the byproduct of a job of spading we had done in the kitchen garden.

Many times my dog Brita and I would climb the gate to the pasture and walk down the cow path across the upper field to the brook. It was quiet and restful there; dragonflies buzzed about the pools and a rare leaf floated down to the water from the overhanging trees. At the bend of the stream a weeping willow leaned far out over the water. Here a deep pool had been washed out and here the biggest shiners and sunfish lay. While the dog investigated the latest messages in the skunk and groundhog holes along the bank, we cut a willow pole and tied on the line, using a ketchup bottle cork for a bobber.

All the long afternoon, as the shadows lengthened across the pole, we sat and watched the bobber, hoping for the big one that I never caught. Chore time came too soon and reluctantly we crossed the meadow again, carrying a half-dozen small fry strung on a piece of packing string. That evening an indulgent mother served them, crisp and brown. We ate them, tails, fins and bones.

## The Old Gristmill

The old gristmills, windmills and sawmills were as characteristic of our early New Hampshire towns as the town hall and white clapboard community churches. "There is probably no country in the world where millstreams are so numerous and universally dispersed or gristmills and sawmills so universally erected as in New England," observed Timothy Dwight in 1796.

The old mills ground Indian corn or maize, for it was the staple nourishment of the New Hampshire folks during the time of the early settlements.

The early farmers were quite thrifty. They only ground a week's worth of meal at a time so as to provide the freshest meal possible; thus the visit to the mill was as regular to them as our weekly trip to the general store. The farmers loitered and gossiped as they waited for their weekly meal, making the mill the village social center of the town.

The old Yankees were very quick to complain, particularly if things were not to their liking. An excerpt from the *Old Mill News* reads:

> *Sundry of the town complained that they cannot get their corn ground at the mill, but that if it must lie there so long as their families suffer*

The perfect brook for fishing—the Ammi Brook in Henniker, New Hampshire, 1940s.

The old mill and log cabin on Lake Kanasatka, Mountonboro, New Hampshire. *Drawing by William H. Bartlett, circa 1834.*

> *for want of it, or they must go so often for it, as some said, it stood them in more carrying and fetching than the corn is worth, which is conceived to come partly by the mill's going so slowly, and partly by the millers not grinding sometimes in the night when he had much work there; wherefore the town desired that the committee before named take some course that this grievance may be removed.*

According to William F. Robinson in his publication *Abandoned New England*, published by the New York Graphic Society, "The village miller was considered the expert in all matters political, legal and mechanical, and his business proficiency made him the most respected man in the village." The miller probably built his own mill, which was made of wood, brick or stone. The mill was usually two stories high including an attic, with a door opening on each floor with ample windows for ventilation. The highest door had a hoist above it for lifting the meal sacks onto the farmers' wagons. The top floor was for storage, and on the first floor was found the grindstone. In the basement stood the great wooden shafts and gears that turned the grindstone.

Today, however, the old gristmill is probably the most commercialized landmark of colonial history. Antique shops, gifts shops and even restaurants inhabit many of these old mills, and those that stand unused are usually found isolated on the back roads near a mountain stream. The legacy of the old mill reminds us of the earlier days in the villages of New Hampshire.

## Stump Pulling

During my younger days, about fifty years ago, I spent many summers in a small town in southern New Hampshire. There was a constant reminder of pioneer days around my grandfather's farm, which can hardly be seen anymore. It was a stump fence. The pasture adjoining the farm had a fence measuring six to eight feet high and tight enough to include or exclude the cows and their relatives. The stumps had been pulled up by previous owners, and they apparently had two problems: How to fence the field and what to do with the stumps—the birth of a fence.

Despite what the advertisement in the *Farm Journal* said, "stump pulling was on its way out." Dynamite was speeding up the process, but all around our land was a stump fence, which appeared rather unique to my city eyes. I never did get the full effect of the figure of speech, which said that she was as "homely as a stump fence."

I remember burning wood in all the stoves and the most effective wood for this purpose was cut from these stumps. Generally, it was cut with a hatchet and later with an axe. It was quick and ideal fuel. It had been drying for more than a lifetime of the oldest inhabitant, and the pitch in the knots was still there as nature intended. My grandfather cut wood for better than twenty years until he had used up all the stumps.

A practical method of removing stumps was to take a pair of oxen or horses and hitch them to the stump. While they pulled, the men cut any roots that showed within reach. Oxen were far better for this type of work than horses, as they were not so temperamental and put steadier pressure on the stump. Every root that was cut let the oxen move the stump a few inches and this encouraged everyone on the detail. Finally the stump might be pulled out of the ground.

Of course, dynamite was the answer for the impatient landowner and if anyone could afford the expense, most anything could be moved. However, dynamite did not get the roots out. Many were left in the ground with the hope that they would rot, but when the old-timers tried to plow the land with a light team, they often caught the plow on roots, which made plowing almost impossible. The roots, which threw the plows out of the furrow, were thrown out by the larger plow with less strain on the horses. With each succeeding plowing it became easier and soon the farmers forgot that there had ever been an obstacle.

I'm sure you have seen men working on new highway construction encountering stumps like those, which caused a lot of trouble in past years. Instead of the verbal exhortation and the lashing of the whip over the backs of the horses, the operator nonchalantly worked the scoop under the stump and the power of a thousand horses lifted it out as easily as lifting an empty grain sack.

The bitter fact was soon borne on the early farmers. Once the land was finally cleared, it wasn't worth a tinker's damn—unless you were going to farm granite stone instead of vegetables. The blossom of nature and her beauty, the clear warm air, the chirping of the birds and the almanac all announce to us that spring is a time for fence building.

## FENCE BUILDING

The post-and-rail was considered by the country folk as the height of sophistication, a model to be admired but seldom copied.

The earlier established farms were usually fenced with the stumps of the great pine trees that once covered the meadows. These had been cut down, sawed into boards, made into shingles or rafted down the river to become "fit masts for some tall admiral."

The fences were made by placing these stumps—extracted from the ground with great labor—on their sides, with their gnarled roots stretching into the air, to form a chevaux de frise that few animals would venture to jump over, but which, with an occasional tear of the trousers, the young were able to climb.

There was, of course, the log fence. This structure was more substantial than the early brush or pole fence, but belonged to the early vintage of our settlers. The great logs, generally pine, were laid straight, overlapping a bit at the ends, on which were placed horizontally the short cross-pieces that held up the logs next above one another. These barricades were usually built three tiers high and formed a very solid wall.

Soon came the rail fence or snake fence. They were so named due to the resemblance of its zigzag line to the shape of a snake. Some natives referred to them as the Virginia fence, named for the common Virginia

Pictured is the upper pasture with Mount Washington in the far distance, as seen from Sugar Hill, New Hampshire, 1940s. The fence is the half wall and half board rest on cross-stakes.

deer. Whether it be rail, snake or Virginia, it is truly American at any rate. This type of fence probably has enclosed more acres of our land than any other type of fence.

Imagine each fence cemented with mosses and enwrapped with vines, so weather-beaten with lichens that not a sliver can be taken from it and not be missed. Take this beauty and add the berry bushes and stones that were pitched into its corners hundreds of years ago.

The child who has not had a rail fence to play on has certainly been deprived of nature's pure happiness. They are so easy to climb and so pleasant to sit upon when there is a flattop rail available.

The fence, which is half wall and half board, has the rural look, resting on cross-stakes slanted across the wall. The end, resting in rough cuts in posts that are built into this, our "post and rail" fence.

The most enduring fence, however, may be considered the traditional stone wall. The foundation is well laid and may surely last as long as the earth itself. This wall soon gets rid of its original look. It may slowly sink or accumulate layers of debris, but it will still be a wall—a ridge of moss and grass, but still a core of stone.

During the building of these walls and fences, consider the bending and straining of the early settlers and the tireless labors of their muscles, the shouting of the oxen and the crude engineering to span their acreage.

The least of all our fences might be said to be the little pickets of slivers that guard the vegetable garden or melon patch from the claws of the wild fowls. These fences maintain their posts until early summer, when the vines have grown strong enough to take care of themselves.

## Changing Seasons

There is something rather special about autumn that sets it apart from other seasons. Perhaps it is that certain briskness in the air when the soft blue mist hovers over the fields and brown hills, or the crisp starlit evenings when the chill breeze sweeps through the meadow in the upland pasture. This is off-season for the farmer and the quiet somber spirit of the time, which gives a welcome sense of leisure after the summer rush of harvest.

Squirrels and chipmunks quickly scamper along the stone walls, gathering up their winter stock of food. The fowl begin to assemble for their fall conventions in the barren fields. Along the roadside, sumacs hold their colorful scarlet banners proudly in the air and blue asters lift their brilliance majestically to the sun. In the swamps, the rigid spikes of cattails begin to change their deep brown cylindrical heads to the light brown, which will be worn as their winter coat. Scattered over the hillside in small schools are the maples and scrub oaks adorning a flaming bouquet of red leaves announcing the bridge of seasons.

This is a time of quiet waiting and reflection, but for apple picking it is a time to pause a moment to look over the land from the vantage point high on the ladder. There is a brooding spirit of season's ending, but a good harvest of Baldwins, Russets, McIntosh and the Northern Spies.

These apples are fine for pies and the like, but cider is our product, and the best is made from the McIntosh. One doesn't say that good cider cannot be made from the sport apple tree that a Scotchman in Canada developed into a variety. If the Macs are picked early while they still have zest, a very fine liquid can be extracted from them. The best cider is a blend in equal proportions of Baldwins, Northern

Halfway Brook with Red Hill in the distance. Moultonboro, New Hampshire, in the 1940s.

Spies and Blue Pearmains. This liquid is colored amber-gold and is not bittersweet.

The old-fashioned apple varieties are gradually disappearing from our landscape, but the wiser farmers will keep a few trees to produce a sweet cider that satisfies the most discriminating taste.

This season is a beautiful interlude between summer and winter and apple picking is one of the enjoyable tasks before the king of the northland sends his legions of snow and cold.

## Late September

It is September, and the apple sweetens and swells upon the bough, the yellow pumpkins glow in the fields and from the fields and barns animals begin to fill out with their first winter fat. The grains are in the stack and dry in the bins and the hay is in the mow.

The crops have been planted and we wait for the harvest. The time of great toil is over and there is only the gathering and storing before winter comes. Yet there is a strange restlessness, for there is a concern, rooted from the past when man and animal feared the uncertainties that winter

A schoolyard game of tag.

brought. We watch and wait and save more than we need. Animals are pressing against time to store food or fat for the lean months.

Pastures are brown and bare and the stock are given a few extra ears of corn each day. Mother searches her kitchen garden for a late tomato or a head of cabbage; it is the tender turnip, which appears on the supper table.

With the first cold rains of fall, the manure pile in back of the barn is hauled to the field that will be in the corn next spring.

Just before the early frosts, turnips, carrots and late cabbage are taken up and carried to the root cellar or buried under an insulation of corn stalk, straw and two feet of earth in the garden. The cabbage is brought in from the garden in baskets, trimmed and washed. Neighboring women help, taking turns at cutting and packing in ten-gallon earthen jars. The heavy jars are carried to the cellar, where in course of time, nature's chemistry will work the change that makes sweet, crisp cabbage leaves into the sour delicacy.

School opens this month and the new teacher finds a room with a family near the schoolhouse. The kids grumble as they force their reluctant feet into unaccustomed shoes, but they are excited at the prospect of seeing old friends again. They march off to the district school with their lunchboxes and slates. Mothers welcome their absence after a summer of having them under their feet all day. A new schedule of after-school duties is posted in the kitchen.

The first spelling bee of the season packs the community into the schoolhouse and little Millie Flanders, an eighth-grade prodigy, spells down Ms. Thelma Brackett, who has been the champion since she was in the eighth grade herself. The air becomes heavy with the fumes of the oil lanterns loaned for the occasion. Tired men and women nod and doze, while they are soothed by the monotones of the spellers around the walls.

September comes to a close with the brisk air of autumn, the overture to winter on the New Hampshire homestead. It is time to finish the general maintenance around the barn and shed, for it is that time of year to harvest the hay on the upper pasture.

## A Time to Scythe the Fields

The history of our New Hampshire towns was written in the soil. Crops of corn, barley, oats and potatoes yielded abundant produce, so the farmer had a margin to dispose of it at the markets in the southern towns. Perhaps the liveliest season in the year was during haying time, when it was the custom to rise with sun, and when, with the scythe swinging upon the arm, the farmer went forth to begin the day's labor in the hayfield. The thoughts of those days are scented with the aroma of new-mown hay.

Those were the times when the whirr and clatter of the mowing machine had not begun to awaken the grass-grown hillsides. Those were the long days of earnest toil, frequently lingering into the hours of late evening before the last of the hay was drawn into the barn by the oxen.

Usually someone would strike in upon the nearest side about midway of the upper field and mow a swath across to the farther side, followed by his partner in regular order. Upon reaching a given point, all would stop and sharpen their scythes. Once the scythes were properly sharpened, the leader would start upon his return, cutting now what was known as the double swath.

The afternoon was filled with raking the sun-cured hay and gathering it into conical piles known as cocks, and by four the oxen were yoked and hitched to the hayrack. One man was delegated to make the load,

John Flanders in buggy with Charles Robinson standing by the horse, Plymouth, New Hampshire, 1920s.

The orchard in Bear Camp Valley.

while another pitched the hay on the cart and a third, usually a boy or girl, raked together the scattering.

What hustling there was when a huge thunderhead pushed its black figure above the rim of the Squam Mountain Range, threatening a summer shower! Now the farmer would give all his attention to the oxen, keeping them mowing from heap to heap of hay while the man with the fork stacked the load on the cart. Just as the big drops began to fall, the last cock was tumbled on the high load, and the oxen started at a dogtrot for the barn.

Perhaps the load would be so high that the barn beam would sweep off a good portion of the hay as the load surged through the doorway. A brief rest followed, lying on the sweetly scented hay, listening to the downpouring of the rain upon the barn's tin roof.

## Apple Cider

Just before the first frost we picked the choice apples from the back orchard, stored them in barrels in the cellar and loaded them into the box bed of our farm wagon for the annual trip to the cider mill. My older brother and I needed no prodding on this job. The Winesaps, Pippins, McIntosh, Northern Spies, Jonathans, Russets, Rambos and even the lowly Ben Davis—a good keeper but without sweetness—were thrown together into the wagon. It was thought that late apples made the best cider and they should be fully ripe and juicy. As we loaded the apples we threw out the mushy ones.

As we jolted along the dusty pike road in the warm autumn sun, the delicate aroma of the delicious and musty tang of the Russet apples lifted around us. The apple smell clung to our bodies and clothes.

At the cider mill, the wagon pulled up at the end of the waiting line of loaded wagons. The aroma of fresh apples was enhanced by the fermenting heap behind the old village mill. There was a tin cup there, but we shunned this, for we had brought along our own supply of rye straws. Inserted in the bunghole, a straw was our preferred method of bringing cider to lip. When our bellies got tight we had to stop, but cider tasted good even after you were full.

The purpose of making cider in the old days was not primarily to supply a delightful beverage; cider was made then to supple the farm vinegar. Farmers have always found it difficult to keep sweet cider for any length of time. So those who wanted both vinegar and a drink made two barrels. The drinking cider was rolled into the cellar, a spigot hammered into one end and a tin cup hung on a convenient nail. Then the family went on an apple juice spree.

The barrel reserved for vinegar was rolled to the sunny side of the kitchen and there it remained until nature had taken her course with it. Then it was spigoted, set up on a platform and referred to daily.

As soon as the cider was in the barrel it gradually lost its delicate flavor, some of the sugar changed to starch and it started to ferment. By the next morning, in warm weather, there would be a thin layer of bubbles on the top—the bacteria had started to multiply and fermentation would progress rapidly. The taste took on a snap, which pleasantly tantalized the taste buds. Within a week, the alcoholic content would go to 6 percent; sweetened apple cider will go to 11 percent alcohol.

A warning must be given, for this is "hard" cider. The temperance societies warn that here we have an alcoholic beverage.

As the alcoholic content reaches its maximum, another change sets in. The hard cider starts to sour. A stringy mass forms, composed of vinegar yeast. Cider vinegar can be kept for a year or so if tightly capped; otherwise it loses its strength.

Cider is made today in much the same way as it has always been made; apples are reduced to a pulp and the juice squeezed from the fruit. During the earlier days, farmers with small orchards had hand presses of their own, but the community mill got the bulk of the crop.

The hand presses were simple. There was a grinder, used to chew up the apples, and a press, operated by a screw, both mounted on a wooden stand. The large presses had greater capacity, for water or steam power was substituted for hand power. The chief drawback of the small hand press is that it will not exhaust the pulp of all its juices. The first juice from a run is released as the apples are ground. As the pressure increases, the juice gets heavier and more flavorful.

Cider made from a mixture of apples is better than that made from a single variety. For example, the juice from the Grimes Golden is bland and almost colorless. Juice from the Delicious is very sweet.

At a power cider mill, the apples are scooped into a hopper. From there they are carried by a chain or belt conveyor to the grinder. The resultant mass of juice is about the consistency of thick applesauce. A decayed spot in an apple discolors the cider and damages the flavor.

Today the apples are thoroughly cleaned under high-pressure water, which also eliminates most of the danger from residual sprays.

From the grinder, or chopper, the pulp falls into a bin directly above the press and awaits the pressing operation.

According to R.J. McGinnis in *The Good Old Days,*

> *A slatted wooden board is placed on the platform of the press, and a frame, with sides several inches high, set on the board. Then a cloth, made of burlap or similar material, is laid over the frame and the pulp is allowed to run out until the frame is heaping full. The cloth is folded over the pulp, corner-wise. Then the frame is lifted off, another slat board is placed over the first layer of pulp, followed by the frame and another cloth. The capacity of a hand press is 6 to 8 layers; that of a power press, 8 to 20 layers. This stack of prepared pulp is called a "cheese." The press is then set in operation, squeezing the juice out between the slatted boards and through the cloth. The juice runs into a trough at the base and thence into a barrel or tank.*

After the cheese is devoid of its juices it is shaken out of the cloth. Today, the pumice is used as cow or hog feed. It is a legend that in one of the heaps of pumice, a "sport" seedling, later to produce the first Delicious apple, grew up.

## The Iron Foundry

Were you aware that we had an iron foundry in the White Mountains of New Hampshire? Our early settlers in constant need of firearms, cooking utensils, nails and other hardware—such as latches and hinges—quickly dotted the landscape with little ironworks. Of course, we immediately think of Pennsylvania as being the original source of iron, but here in New Hampshire, foundries were established and ran at a profit for several years.

In Richard Allen's article "Furnaces, Forges, and Foundries in Vermont, 1956–57," he writes, "The period of growth of these deposits is supposed to be about twenty-five years, and it is found in various depths of water from two to twenty feet. A man accustomed to the employment being in a small boat, with an instrument similar to oyster tongs, can raise from its watery bed about half a ton of ore a day."

The iron furnace located beside the river in Franconia, New Hampshire. The furnace is built of stone. The stack is approximately forty feet high. Just in back of the tower there are traces of the road down the embankment where the ore was hauled from Iron Mountain, or Ore Hill, as it was then called, circa 1800s.

In 1811, the company employed ten men to blast out the ore and transport it downhill to the blast furnace. For several years, until 1849, they mined the well. The mountainside had a vertical slice cut out of it measuring 660 feet long, 144 feet deep and about 4 feet wide.

Production grew to the point where they produced finished items such as nails, kettles, a sundry of tools and the famous Franconia Stove. At the height of production, the company employed fifty men on a yearly basis, and another fifty when the large furnace was actually in full blast.

John Spargo's "Iron and Smelting in Bennington, Vermont," 1938, provides the following:

> *Generally, the autumn and winter months are chosen to put the furnace in blast, the workmen then being obtained at lower wages* [as there was no competition for farm labor this time of year] *and the outdoor workmen being called in. It has been ascertained also, that a larger quantity of iron is reduced in a given time, in the winter months, which is supposed to be dependent on the more condensed and drier state of the atmosphere, by which the nature of the blast is modified, while the draught of the furnace is also affected by the heated gasses and the surrounding air.*

In spite of their high quality, the Franconia Furnace simply could not compete with the more accessible furnaces farther south, where better transportation was provided them. Gradually the labor force was reduced, until 1865 when the foundry was forced to close. In 1884, fire completely gutted the old buildings, leaving only the blast furnace to stand beside the Gale River.

The local forges have vanished and the only remains are the small dam sites and spillways that powered the waterwheels. So now, the roar of the furnace, the pounding of machinery and the belching smoke is no longer visible in the mountains. The Salisbury Iron Region, Franconia and Katahdin are all quiet rural hamlets with only the monolithic furnace stacks to remind us of the bygone days. Our memory lingers on, our legacy established, but the epitaph is written.

## Winter in the North Country

How muffled is the land in its raiment that in nature comes the voice that life continues beneath the semblance of deep sleep, that her warm heart still beats under the white cover of winter. So disguised in whiteness that familiar places are strange, rough hollows smoothed to mere undulations, deceitful to the eye, and level fields so filled with heaps and ridges that their owners scarcely recognize them. The most rustic fence is a hedge of pearl finer than a wall of marble, and the meanest wayside weed is a white flower of magical charm.

Take a walk on a mountain path and listen to the slow, smothered trickle coming from the mountain stream through its double roofing of snow and ice. The forest, which the winter freeze and winds stripped of its leafy branches, is roofed again with an ornamentation of alabaster more delicate than the green canopy that summer unfolds, and the floor is set in noiseless pavement, traced with a shifting pattern of blue shadows.

Notice that beneath its frozen plains, the lakes bewail their imprisonment with hollow moans awakening a wild and mournful chorus of echoes from sleeping shores that answer now no caress of ripples nor angry stroke of waves or the dip and splash of the boatman's oar and paddle.

Wild game wallow through the snow, a crumbling furrow that obliterates identity of either trail, yet there are tracks that tell as plain as written words had made them. Here have fallen, light as snowflakes,

A winter scene in the Flume at Franconia Notch in the White Mountains, New Hampshire, 1930s.

the broad pads of the hare, white as the snow he trod; there, the parallel tracks of another winter squirrel, linking from tree to tree. The leaps of a small wood mouse are lightly marked upon the feathery surface to where there is the imprint of a light, swift pinion on either side, and the little story of the wandering ends—one crimson blood drop, the period that marks the finish. Amid all the desolation of their woodland haunts, the squirrels voice their delight in windless days of sunshine, and scoff at biting cold and wintry blasts.

In the blue shadow at the bottom of that winding brook are the delicate prints of a grouse. Marsh and forest brooks are scarcely distinguishable, but by the white domes of the muskrats' winter homes, and here and there a sprawling bush, for the growth of weeds is beaten flat, the deep snow covers it and the channel ice is one unbroken sheet.

The bays and coves of Winnipesaukee are frozen and the remaining open water, black beneath clouds or bluer than the blue dome that arches it, looks as cold as ice and snow. Sometimes its steaming breath lies close above it, sometimes mounts in swaying, lofty columns to the sky, but always cold and ghostly, without expression of life.

So far away, to majestic peaks that shine with a glittering gleam against the blue rim of the sky, stretches the universal whiteness. It coldly shines the sun from the low curve of its course, and so chilled comes the lightest waft of wind from the north, that it takes the imagination to picture any land on all the earth where spring is just awakening fresh life, and of warm waves on pleasant shores.

Now, at the close of a white winter's day, the sunset paints a promise and prophecy in a blaze of color on the heavens. The gray clouds kindle with red and yellow fire that burns about their purple hearts in tints of infinite variety, while behind them the dark blue landscape of the Chocorua Mountain frames the lost glory of the departing sun, fading in the tint of tender green to the upper blue. The cold snow at our feet flushes with warm color, and the eastern hills blush roseate against the climbing, darkening shadows of the valley.

Night, under cloudy skies or silvering her face with the evening light of moon and stars, brings other mysterious voices. Solemnly the unearthly voices of the owl resound from his woodland hermitage. The fox's gasping bark marks his wayward course across the frozen fields on some errand of love. Swelling and falling with the lapse of the night wind come from the mountain ridges the baying of hounds, hunting alone and unheeded, while the master basks in the comfort of his fireside.

The land, whose brightness has never been told, lies unveiled before us. Its majestic mountains, spectacular with innumerable hues; its lakes and streams of gold, rippling to purple shores, seem not to be so far from us, but that we might, by a short journey, come to them.

## A Climb up Whiteface Mountain

Boldly standing in the Sandwich Mountain Range, with its solid bulk thrust well forward in advance of its neighbors, is Whiteface Mountain. East of the mountain is the rounded footstool of Wonalancet, followed by the craggy, rough mass of Paugus and finally the white pinnacle of Chocorua, where the range abruptly ends. In the southwest is an elevated plateau beyond which rises the broad expanse of Sandwich Dome. To the rear and northwest is the majestic saw-toothed Tripyramid, while to the northeast rises the dark and symmetrical Passaconaway.

In this group of distinctive summits, Whiteface looms forth as a mountain of impressive bulk. As we view it from the south, there is seen a broad scar that exposes the bedrock of the mountain below its summit, giving it a characteristic appearance, which in turn became responsible for its name. As we view it from other mountains to the north, we cannot see the scar and the summit takes on an altered look, appearing as if lightly notched. In character the mountain is the very opposite of Chocorua. Whiteface gives the appearance of a broad, massive and masculine mountain, whereas Mount Chocorua is slender, pointed and almost feminine.

This is a mountain that is a must for climbers. It is readily accessible by automobile, but lies several miles from the principal arteries of travel. The east side trunk line of the New Hampshire highway system is ten miles away.

The trail I used began at Wonalancet Intervale. In the Intervale, a road will be found running northwest to Ferncroft, which is at the farther margin of the wide fields and pastures. A road forks from this immediately beyond Ferncroft, crosses Swift River on the Squirrel Bridge, bends to the right beyond the bridge and presently passes in front of a cottage that stands on the right in an opening. Just beyond this point a path leads through a gate in a fence and gradually begins to ascend. Presently the trail forks. Here the old road turns to the left and continues to Whiteface Intervale, southwest from this point. The path to the right, which is the one that you want to take, is the Blueberry Ledge Trail to the summit of Whiteface.

The trail soon crosses a marshy area where it then begins a steady ascent, and approximately a mile from Ferncroft crosses the open ledges that give the trail its name. Here we get our first panorama of country to the south and southeast. The ledges slope gently, with hollows and grassy terraces with only a few clumps of trees clustered about the landscape.

At the upper margin of the ledges, the trail enters thick woods and soon begins to climb steadily through a hardwood forest, with vistas in every direction. While this part of the trail is free from precipitous rocks, the way is nevertheless rather steep in many places. After about a mile and a quarter, we approach an opening known as Wonalancet Outlook, which gives a limited view toward the southeast. Our altitude at this point is approximately three thousand feet.

Soon the trail enters the woods and ascends steeply until it reaches the crest of the spur. Here there is a short stretch of downhill grade into a little hollow that lies at the foot of the final rocky climb to the summit. At this point we have a rather fine view of the summit through the trees, very much enlarged as to details and still appearing to represent a considerable climb.

We now begin the final—and possibly most interesting—part of our climb. A brief way above this point, the trail clambers over a series of ledges like big rock steps. In ascending, the path zigzags back and forth, across the rocky terraces. We are now on the backbone ridge of the mountain. To the right we have an occasional glimpse of a deep, round valley, on the farther side of which rises the high, dark cone of Passaconaway. To the left are openings from which we can look across the huge rock cliff of Whiteface, falling at a steep angle from the summit to the deep valley that lies below.

The face of the mountain was laid bare by an enormous slide that occurred in the fall of 1820. Thousands of tons of earth, trees and rocks, made unstable by the rains, slid down into the valley. On the face of the bedrock, a few bushes and small trees have since found footing where seams or crevices serve to catch and hold a little soil. For the most part, the rocks have remained gaunt and smooth, and the effect, as we look across this wide area and down the steep, sheer drop, is one that will not soon be forgotten.

The real summit of the mountain lies to the northwest, a short distance from the area above the cliff. The open rock where the trail emerges is commonly spoken of as the summit; here, the open vistas of the surrounding landscape may be experienced.

From the summit of Whiteface, a high ridge describes an arc to the north and then to the east connecting the two mountains. Directly across from Whiteface toward Passaconaway, the mountain masses drop away in a round, heavily forest valley known as the Bowl.

To the right from Passaconaway extends another high ridge that rises in two prominent summits and then joins a lesser mountain mass that swings around toward the southwest over three eminencies known as Mounts Hedgehog, Hubbard and Wonalancet. The last of these three is the final outpost of the long and lofty ridge. Its sides drop sharply away into the valley in the direction of Ferncroft. The summit of this outpost is a little south of east from the summit of Whiteface. Over the undulating ridge that swings southeast from Passaconaway are seen the ragged summits of Moat Mountain, near North Conway, and over these rises the summit of Kearsarge. Paugus and Chocorua lie due north of east from Whiteface.

Looking in an easterly direction, several lakes are visible: Chocorua, the Conway Lakes and Silver Lake. In the direction of Conway Lake and beyond are seen distant lakes in Maine, near which rises the low, long bulk of Pleasant Mountain.

In the southeast, to the right of Silver Lake, is Ossipee Lake, backed by Green Mountain. Close by, in the direction of Great Hill Pond, are the dark summits of the Ossipee Mountains. Just to the right of the Ossipees is Lake Winnipesaukee with its seventy-two-square-mile sheet of water, and beyond the lake is the Belknap Mountain Range. To the right is Red Hill and Squam Lake. If the visibility is clear, Mount Kearsarge, in Warner, may be seen over the right margin of Squam Lake. Sandwich Mountain is a little to the right of southeast and is somewhat more than five miles distant. Farther to the right is Mount Tecumseh in the Waterville Valley, and over Tecumseh lies Moosilauke.

Looking northward may be seen the Presidential Range, with Mount Washington commanding the range. To the left of Washington is the small and jagged summit of Mount Monroe, greatly dwarfed by distance, and, again to the left is the rounded dome of Mount Pleasant. Between Monroe and Pleasant, the peak of Mount Jefferson

A climb up Whiteface Mountain in the winter.

stands majestically against the skyline. To the right is a part of the Montalban Ridge, including the Giant Stairs, with Mount Resolution on the right and Mount Crawford on the left. Farther away on the right of Mount Washington are the summits of the Carter-Moriah Range.

After spending some quiet moments viewing the magnificent landscape, we make our return to the valley. The easier path is possibly the Blueberry Ledge Trail, by which we ascended. The steeper and more difficult is the Tom Wiggin Trail.

The Blueberry Ledge Trail will take us over the crest of the wooded knoll and on the farther side will descend at a sharp angle through the hardwood forest. After a time we will come out on the upper margin of the Blueberry Ridge and will follow the trail as it meanders across to the lower margin. Entering the woods again beyond the ledges, we will have a rather easy route for the rest of our journey. As we near the base of the spur, the trail from Whiteface Intervale will be found coming in on the right. Soon we will pass through the gate and come out into the opening at the end of the road that crosses the Squirrel Bridge.

This is a good mountain to hike, for the trail skirts an impressive cliff and commanding views of the surrounding mountains, lakes and valleys. The round trip to the summit of Whiteface can be done in six hours of steady climbing, but I would allow seven or eight in order to have ample time on the summit—it is time well spent!

## Ice Harvesting

Icehouses, once commonplace on the better farms throughout the state, have with few exceptions disappeared from our landscape. The decline set in about eighty years ago when the mechanical refrigerators and power lines began to come into the countryside. There are few, if any, survivors in New England.

Ice harvesting usually came toward the end of January or early February, when the ice was about ten inches thick. The best temperature for cutting was a few degrees below freezing, so the water would freeze quickly on the cakes after they were taken out of the lakes or ponds. But it seemed that it never was a pleasant twenty-five degrees; frequently it was zero or below. Men did not dare to wait, for too often a zero spell in New Hampshire was followed by a thaw that would spoil the ice.

After the snow was scraped from an area, the ice was plowed out. The ice plow was a weighted, horse-drawn contrivance with a row of sharp teeth that cut a narrow furrow six or seven inches deep. A marker scratched a line for the next cut. The plow was run one way over an area, then over the other at right angles, plowing out a checkerboard pattern of cakes of a more or less standard size, twenty-two inches by twelve inches, weighing about a hundred pounds. Sometimes the cakes were broken apart with a bar, but particular people liked to have the edges smooth, so the last two or three inches were sawed by hand. The ice saw was straight bladed and four or five feet in length with a handle like a lawn mower.

After the cakes were cut, they were poled through the water to the shore. Here a long plank sloped into the water. The trick was to give the cake of ice enough momentum so that its weight would carry it up where someone with a pair of tongs could snag it. It seems that every year someone would fall in; he either lost his footing or his pole skidded. He would be fished out, rushed to the nearest house and hustled into the kitchen to warm by a crackling fire. Finally, this was followed by two or three cups of strong coffee, a treatment pleasant enough to make him consider falling in purposely.

A century ago the ice was hauled to the icehouse on two-horse bobsleds. Layer by layer the old weathered icehouse was filled. A sprinkling of dry sawdust was scattered between each layer of cakes. This made them easier to separate when they were taken out. A two-foot-wide layer of sawdust was tamped lightly between the ice and the sides of the building. After the last layer was pushed up the long, oak plank, the whole heap was covered a yard deep with sawdust.

Some farmers not only cut ice for their own needs, but also supplied it for neighbors. The going price was five cents a cake. But the thrifty farmers owned their own ice-cutting equipment. It took an average of three hundred cakes to last a family through the summer; at five cents a cake this was fifteen dollars, one-third the price of a good cow.

Time was when ice harvesting was a major industry in the Lakes Region. No one knows exactly when a farsighted colonial farmer first conceived the idea of storing ice to use in hot weather. Old records reveal that many icehouses were built in New England after the Revolution. An entry in George Washington's diary indicates that he stored ice in winter. The diary, dated 1785, reads, "Having put the heavy frame into my Ice House, I began this day to seal it with Boards."

As towns grew into cities during the first half of the nineteenth century, the demand for ice grew rapidly. Within a few miles of the major population centers, gigantic rough-board icehouses were built on the shores of our ponds, lakes and rivers. Ice for Concord and Boston were cut on Lake Winnipesaukee and stored in the Lakeport Icehouse. During the late nineteenth and early twentieth centuries, ice was transported to these cities via rail or truck.

Ice became a spectacular item of international commerce. In 1805, Frederick Tudor of Boston conceived the idea of sending ice by ship to the West Indies, where ice had never been used. In the next thirty years, Tudor made a fortune shipping the cold luxury to the West and the East Indies, to South America, China and England. In 1853, A.J. Downing, one of America's famous pioneer landscape architects, wrote, "American ice has sent into positive ecstasies all those of the great metropolis [London] who depend upon their throats for sensations."

Commercial ice harvesting has become a thing of the past, a memory of the good old days.

Cutting ice, Wolfeboro Bay, 1996. *Photograph Courtesy of Breakwind Farms, LLC, Freedom, New Hampshire.*

## ICE FISHING ON THE BIG LAKE

Ice fishing in New Hampshire has long been a way of winter life, and it is here that great hordes of people congregate on the ice to enjoy this recreation and to exchange pleasantries with other winter fishermen. The lake is stocked with salmon, which are taken from early spring through the summer months. Lake trout, native to the lake, are caught from January 1 through September 30. Smelt, whitefish, small mouth bass, yellow perch, horned pout, suckers and chain pickerel are all taken in season.

I have had many visitors to the Lakes Region ask, "What enjoyment do these people get from ice fishing in those shanties? How do they know where the best fishing is on such a large lake, and why, for Pete's sake, do they call them 'Bob houses'?"

Contrary to the seclusion desired by the summertime fisherman, ice fishermen seem to be a friendly lot. They delight in visiting together and sharing fishing lore. Very few will object if you walk from group to group, asking questions. When you see a group of fishermen and women huddled together out on the ice, you can be sure of two things: there is a lot of idle chatting going on, and there's probably a good school of fish right below them, waiting to be caught.

If you are a first-timer at the sport, probably your best bet in determining where to go ice fishing is to experiment at first and go with the crowd, but more important, go with someone who knows what he is doing. As I mentioned earlier, most successful fishermen don't mind sharing their secrets, and many old-timers derive great pleasure from helping a newcomer acquire skill. When you tell your friend you're seeking the advantages of his experience and success, he's bound to be willing to show you the techniques of good ice fishing.

There are exceptions to this, of course. A few old-timers take their ice fishing so seriously that they resent any intrusion into their fishing time. Don't feel bad if someone tells you to get lost, for the next person you ask might take a real interest in you, and in the long run you'll be a better fisherman than the guy who was too proud to ask—and you may even become better than the guy too busy to help.

If you want to be a good fisherman, you must learn all you can about the proper equipment and techniques used to catch fish. You must be at least as smart as the fish. The old saying about leading a horse to water also applies to fish. You just can't make a fish bite unless it wants to.

Many times I have stood on the shore of the lake in winter and wondered what was going on under that ice cover. I do know that fish are not nearly as active in winter as in summer. During the spring months especially, almost every species of fish is busy spawning, eating and hiding to keep from being eaten by larger fish. During this period fish eat almost everything that moves, including various lures and flies that summertime anglers throw at them. They are even known to chase and strike at lures three times larger then they are.

But in the wintertime, fish act quite differently. The only requirement of fish in the winter is that they eat enough to stay alive. The less they move about, the less food and energy they need to live. So the job of enticing a fish to hit a lure or to move very far to take live bait becomes quite a challenge. I am told, however, that wintertime fishermen catch more fish per man-hour of fishing than summer anglers. The reason for this is that "the ice fisherman can handle more rods and tip-ups, and his average catch per rod goes up," say angler Bennett.

A winter settlement of ice shanties on Wolfeboro Bay, Wolfeboro, New Hampshire. The shanties are typically furnished with home comforts, which add a touch of interest and color to the winter scene.

Generally, fish in the wintertime are quite lethargic, coming out to feed only part of the day. The rest of the time the fish hide in the few weeds left on the bottom of the lake and rest. Weeds that grow tall, even reaching the surface during the summer, recede and fall to the bottom of the lake during freezing weather. Fish that need to hide to stay alive seek cover in these weedy remains; that is the place to search them out.

Each lake's fish population lives according to a fairly stable timetable. Competition for food seems to be the key to fish's feeding habits. Therefore, it stands to reason that if you learn when the fish's movements occur you can save a lot of fishing time.

Another important part of knowing fish is to know their reaction to you. Too many fishermen think that what they do on top of the ice cannot be detected by the fish below. They proceed quite noisily—tearing up the lake with spuds, dropping tools and gear on the ice and, in general, making quite a racket. Sound waves created on top of the ice travel through ice and on through the water just as if they were an electric current. Small fish may move away from all the noise and then turn and come back, but larger fish are much more cautious.

Eventually, after the noise dies down, the fish will recover from their fright and behave normally, In the meantime, you have lost an hour of good fishing. Talking and yelling and other vocal noises are permissible because the sound travels through the air, but for better fishing, keep the mechanics of hole making and shanty building to a minimum.

For many years, ice fishing has been a tradition on our New Hampshire lakes. Shortly after Christmas, ice begins to form across most lakes, and one by one, the ice shanties—Bob houses—appear on the bays, until literally hundreds are scattered across the entire lake. [*Note:* The term "Bob house" came about by the action of the line in the hole of the ice—it "bobs."]

During the past thirty years, the Meredith Rotary Club has sponsored "The Great Rotary Club Fishing Derby" as an annual fundraiser for the many projects of the club. This derby is usually conducted during the first half of February each year and attracts thousands of participants from all over the East Coast of the United States and Canada. So, you see, ice fishing is more than a sport; it is a way of life.

## Spring is Coming

Long before the smallest shoots of green vegetation struggle into sight and the days begin to lengthen in New Hampshire, we patiently await the arrival of spring. Visual confirmation is given by the sight of bare spots on the side of the logs, the corn snow, the first sap run, the rush of the smelt and the muddy dirt roads that weave through the backland.

What can be more pleasing and satisfying to the mind and spirit than a tramp on snowshoes into the suddenly awakened sap orchard? We hear the pizzicato tones of sap dripping into the tin buckets, the hushed startled whirr of the busy chickadees and white-tailed sparrows and the crows cawing in the distance. Our noses share in the renewed pleasures as a deep breath brings to it the aroma of fir balsam, thawing earth and the boiling sweet sap. However, winter is not yet in full retreat! The men on the sleds jogging over snow-hidden hummocks on their trips to and from the warm sap house are heavily dressed and the horses steam in the sun as they doze lazily while gathering pails are emptied and again refilled.

Overhead a chipmunk has proved himself to be no less ingenious and industrious than man in the gathering the sweet nectar. He has gnawed

A mountain stream may be heard as a soft roar while it races to Cold River.

a hole in the bark on the underside of one of the small maple branches, tilted his head backward and is drinking drop by drop.

Let us ramble down to the mountain stream, which is now unfettered from the winter's chains. The mushy snow shows numerous animal tracks, crossed and crisscrossed, some of which are difficult to identify. A lone squirrel has burrowed deep for some nuts he hid last fall. An old decayed stump, pulled apart and surrounded by fresh tracks, tells us that Big Blackie has recently been in search of food to fill his clamoring stomach. Farther, freshly stripped young raspberry canes, interspersed with more familiar tracks, announce this area as a favorite haunt of deer. Then our attention is diverted to a nearby maple of muted, guttural sounds. There, upon further investigation, is seen a large porcupine, methodically stripping and munching bark. Occasionally he rejects a strip in favor of a covenant and more newly swelled buds.

Before reaching the stream, the soft roar of its rushing torrents can be heard. During the summer, our stream is quite small, occasionally gurgling and bubbling as it flows around large granite stones. These small rapids drop and whirl, making the perfect trout pool. We intend to return to this spot in early May with rod and reel to see just how perfect it really is. Today our stream is a scene of seething strength.

Branches, bark and leaves are dashing rapidly downstream, being obstructed by rock and glass sheets of ice clinging to the banks just above the current's reach.

In the open fields snow is still quite visible, except for a skirting around the woodpile and walls. The distant drumming of a partridge is faintly heard, as well as the hammering of an assiduous woodpecker on the hollow tree in the distance.

Trudging homeward, we feel pleasantly tired but refreshed. The sap house is quiet, save the cherry crackle of the last wood supply heaped upon the fire, an occasional clink in the recently emptied buckets and the dripping from the icicles about the eaves of our barn.

There is no easier way of getting rid of cabin fever and renewing spring fever than by taking an early walk in the awakening woods and field of New Hampshire. Spring is now blossoming in New Hampshire.

## Chapter Four

# Village Memories

It was only a little village, but I loved it in those precious days when life surged forward hourly into the work, the play, the misfortunes and the glories among which my family, friends and neighbors moved with sturdy New Hampshire vigor.

Here we live. Hotels with spacious, flowery lawns rose graciously above our Main Street homes with their white clapboards and green blinds—many of them announcing to the travelers the Tavern, The Inn, Sunset Hill, Old Homestead, Mountain Rest and other invitations in which grace and welcome spoke above any mercenary invitations.

Nestled in the peaceful hamlet, not a soul in sight as far as an eye could reach. Where was the homely old blacksmith shop in which I played amid showers of sparks from the resounding anvil? What about the school bell calling the village youth from their game of fox-and-geese in the snow? Remember Christmas Day with its bountiful homemade church supper and the Christmas trees loaded with gifts for all, parlor games 'til twelve and then seeing Helen home? What about the snowshoeing party, which was moving briskly down the field by the power line? Where are the flocks of youngsters racing brightly around the ice pond, some snapping the whip while others turn into the bonfire circle for a warming up? But this is only a corner of my memory.

Who in past generations can recall a dreary hour in the winter of his or her youth? Let us not imply that it was all fun; there was work to be done. Cows had to be milked, horses fed and harnessed, stove wood carried into the shed from under the barn, apple pies made, socks

Wolfeboro's Main Street looking north, circa 1920s. The village, with its spacious homes and white clapboards and green blinds, graces the main street of the town.

mended, paths shoveled, skis waxed, snowshoes repaired, guns cleaned and oiled, skates sharpened, wood and lumber chopped, limbed, yarded and piled.

Remember the old farmhouse? It binds the end of a trailing upward climb of a mile above the village where we may look down among the memorable treasures of yesterday. It nestles under a backdrop of mountains whose beauty changes with every vagary of nature without growing old. The sound of a cow's bell in the meadow lingers in the crisp morning air above the murmur now rising from the village life below. Beyond the grove on the southern slope, the ice pond is a glistening jewel set in green. From this new restoration of our youth we fish, hunt, wander among the hill, work, play, read, write, welcome old friends and just live for fun—a fun that fans the glowing embers of memory into a flame of present jubilation.

## The Town Common, Green or Square

Everyone who knows New Hampshire pictures a quaint village green in its center with its Ionic porticoes, elms, bandstands, honor rolls, white steeples, tavern signs, small-paned windows and green turf. Whatever our picture, it was the center of colonial social life.

Yet any assertion about the village green needs to be qualified. Usually they are triangular, square, round or egg-shaped grassy islands cut away from the central common by diverging roads. In most pictures all the houses are white and their lawns well groomed.

How might we define a village green? We may find justification for giving the name to any open green space jointly owned by a town, a city or a group of individuals.

As we drive through New England, we find that greens vary in size. What was once a wide common may have been pared down to a weedy triangle hardly large enough to contain the Honor Roll of the Second World War, such as that in Veterans' Square in Laconia. Some greens, however, have been protected by public-spirited citizens who have fought to preserve them against the encroachments of progress, so that they may retain some of their old spaciousness. Sometimes the charm of a green lies not in its extent but in its compactness, as is seen in Plymouth, New Hampshire. There is an inevitable quality about such greens; they should be as they are and where they are.

The old records reveal that there was little distinction between greens and commons. According to Mr. Webster, "A common is a place for pleasure, for pasturage." We would like to believe that pleasure was the idea behind these elm-shaded green spaces—there are literally hundreds of them in New England—but we fear our ancestors were thinking mainly of pasturage.

A common, then, is not necessarily a green, although a green is always a common. A green is the center of a community, and many times is in the form of a square. It may be called a common, but still it has about it a feeling of compactness, of neighborliness that belongs to the time when small towns were self-sufficient—weaving wool shorn from their own sheep, grinding their own grain, baking bricks for the occasional mansion house that accents the green and white pattern of the village, making their own harness and saddles from the hides of their own steers.

Local craftsmen built the houses around the greens. Glass for the small-paned windows and for the fanlights over the doors came from a distance, but the timbers and clapboards, shingles and panels once grew on hillsides about the town. The brook, with its blue flags and jewelweed, supplied the power that sawed the boards. The village blacksmith hammered out hinges and latches. If nails were needed, he made them, but many of the old houses were joined almost entirely with wooden pegs. It is natural enough that the houses looked as if they grew out of the ground on which they stand.

Those days, when the blacksmith shoed a horse and then set to work on a strap hinge for somebody's barn door, are long gone. The common is often much older and the underlying reason for its existence may be traced back a thousand years before it gets lost in the mists of antiquity. The English settlers who first came to America brought with them ideas concerning ownership of land that were already old in England when William the Conqueror crossed the channel. The system of agriculture, based on these ideas, came into England with the Angles and Saxons. It was called the common field system. The historian Tacitus found German tribes carrying on farming in this way, which goes back to the time when nomads settled down and had to plan for a fair division of land. First the division was among members of a family; then, as the group increased, between members of a clan; and later among neighbors.

There is a record of how twelve elders of a village organized a community. They began by laying out a village green, which was in the center of the town and was to be used as a night pasture to protect cattle from wolves and thieves. The rest of the land was divided into plough land, meadowland and common. Each household was assigned a piece of the plough land near his house for an orchard. His meadows might be at some distance away. Each holder contained some of the better land and some of the poorer.

The common land belonged to the whole village and all the landholders had certain rights in it. They could lop off the limbs for their own firewood, but not cut down trees and go into the lumber business. They could dig up gravel or clay for their own use, but not sell it. Villagers could remove grass from the common land but only "by the mouths of their cattle"; they could not store it or sell it.

Rights of pasturage used to belong to certain houses in America just as they did in England. We like to imagine the present residents of Boston's Beacon Street in the section opposite Boston Common driving cows to pasture, looping off branches, bringing in wood and cutting turf. In fact, commons, squares or greens are seldom places for pasturage now, but they are still used for pleasure—a pleasure that they offer to every visitor willing to turn aside from main roads and rest a while under their elms. The roots of so many Americans are in these peaceful village

Common and Main Street in Plymouth, New Hampshire, 1905. The common was considered the center for social, political and economic affairs of the community.

commons. They bring us not only a sense of dignity, serenity and quiet beauty, but also of homecoming.

## The Town House

One of the ever-present features of our village is the Town House. As we view this hamlet from afar, the buildings appear huddled together in the valley below as though for common protection. But the Town House, usually a wooden structure painted white, stands out boldly, due partly to its size, but mostly to the solid competence it magnetizes.

In many of our villages, the Town House started its life as a meetinghouse, but in time descended from the spiritual edifice to more worldly affairs, such as furnishing the selectmen with an office, the townspeople with a hall for the annual meetings and local grange suppers and the young folk a place for dances, sports and other forms of entertainment.

The day of the March town meeting has arrived and teams are hitched at the rear in the horse sheds. Quite a number of townsfolk are

The Center Harbor Town House, 1843–1907.

about, going to and coming from the general store, standing in groups, earnestly talking, some rather heatedly. The stripes fly from the tall staff by the inscribed boulder commemorating the village youth who fought in the early wars.

Inside the hall, people are filling up the seats that have been properly lined in neatly assigned rows. They have come down from the snowswept hill farms to vote on various articles in the town warrant, some of which have had their villagers in turmoil for weeks. Gradually the hall fills, the moderator gavels the meeting to order and the town business is in full swing. If anyone feels his road hasn't been satisfactorily tended, the town fathers, or possibly the road agent, hear about it in no uncertain terms. If someone thinks that the selectmen have conducted themselves, during the past year, like three old women, they are so informed.

The selectmen may or may not be listening. Chances are they're in a great conference, rustling important papers or walking about the platform talking with the moderator or tax collector about affairs of state. One by one the articles are disposed of; money is raised and appropriated for a new winter plow or roller, for repairing the covered bridge over Cold River, for the salaries of officers for the ensuing year.

The old hall resounds to a full-throated alternate ayes and nays; the townspeople literally have a voice in their municipal affairs.

The selectmen properly organize after the town meeting. Sitting by their stove in the Town House with the inventory books before them and planning for the coming year, they have more of a knack for running the town than many fluent jittery, super-cultured columnists and holy-minded do-gooders who insist they know how to run the world better than the locals.

The selectmen have no tendency to jump up and down; neither has the Town House. It's been solidly set there for more than a century and a half, and it's likely to be there for a long time to come.

## The Town Pound

It was commonplace during the colonial days to have a central green for the purpose of grazing animals. The livestock of the surrounding farms would be let loose onto the central green, where they would spend the day.

As more and more farms sprang up and the livestock were let loose to graze, more often than not, the animals went beyond the green and spread into another farmer's field and damaged the crops. In order to solve this problem, the communities began to construct town pounds or corrals. Whenever a stray animal was found unattended, it was brought to this corral until the owner claimed and paid for the stray.

We still find these pounds scattered throughout the state. They were usually a rectangular (twenty-five by forty feet) corral, chest high and made entirely of wall-cut granite stone. The gates were made of iron-hinged doors or a few boards held by a pole wedged against them. The location of the pound was just outside the village proper, but far enough away so as not to be a nuisance to the town's people.

Many citizens with political aspirations ran for the position as pound keeper or custodian. Many times this position required the physical wrestling of a stray hog, a runaway bull or other loose animals roving the township. To make matters worse, the pound keeper was liable for the expense of feeding the stray in his care. In many of our towns, the custodial appointment was given to the most recent married young man by vote of the annual town meeting and his compensation would be a set percentage received of the fines collected.

The Town Pound in Center Harbor, New Hampshire, established 1799. "Wherein stray cattle, sheep, horses & pigs were impounded until rightful owner could find his animal and pay a fine." The first pound keeper was W. Jeremiah Towle. The pound is a rectangular corral, chest high and made entirely of wall-cut granite stone.

By the end of the 1800s, many of the town pounds fell into disuse and became obsolete. Today we find some of these vandalized walls leveled into obscure heaps of granite rubble. However, a few have been salvaged by local historical societies and stand as a reminder of our legacy, and there are those that remain in the remote corners of our quiet hamlets as mementos of a legacy of bygone days.

## THE OLDE COUNTRY STORE

It is quiet. Not silent—just pleasantly quiet. Consider the soft silence on an autumn day in the deep woods of New Hampshire, the sad stillness around the old cellar holes, the awkward hush that surges into the busy stagecoach on its way to Conway. But there's no quiet so restful as that of a country store.

One, possibly two, customers are standing by the counter, obviously in no hurry to run off. The proprietor speaks to one of the customers in a low, easy tone. The business seems almost confidential. The order is gradually filled. The proprietor writes down figures on a brown paper package, leisurely adds them up, yawning comfortably, accepts payment and the customer unobtrusively leaves the store.

The second customer is likewise attended to, and he also walks out, not slowly, not fast, just sort of normal.

Now it's your turn. Perhaps all you want are crackers and cheese. Quietly the proprietor slices off the cheese with a large knife and as you eat, you engage him in some political conversation of the day. Not heavy intellectual repartee, just a chat, slow and punctuated by many long pauses. The old clock ticks softly on the wall. A cat naps in the window among the dried fruit. Outside, the Concord Coach arrives to discharge a few passengers.

Axe helves and cant-dogs, lumbermen's stockings and felt boots, candy kisses and cans of beans wait patiently about. A wood chunk in the stove rolls over and the proprietor puts in another log. The fire sings cheerily in the flue. Outside we see it is beginning to flurry.

The Olde Country Store in Moultonboro, New Hampshire. This store has been in business since 1793 as a tavern, post office, stage stop and library. Today you may find the store on Route 25 in the center of town.

Through the door you look up the quiet village street. The stately white houses are set back from the road, widely spaced with the graceful elms and oak trees framing the peaceful road leading to the lake. Only one person is in sight, an old gentleman with a cane. Everything is serene, secure. You feel yourself slowed to a snail's pace, relaxed.

Soon the old gentleman comes in. "It snows," he mutters.

He purchases some smoking tobacco, leisurely fills and lights his pipe and stands quietly gazing up and down the street. No one says anything. The clock goes on ticking; the store goes on living. It will be there tomorrow.

## THE EARLY NEW HAMPSHIRE INNS AND TAVERNS

There were many inns and taverns throughout the state in which the early traveler and farmer could obtain nourishment or room if he needed to warm his bones, stir his tongue and make palatable the half-thawed porridge, which he ate in front of the cheerful tavern fire.

It was the invariable custom to carry a supply of food for his journey. At the inn, however, the traveler did not carry his meals. At the inn he paid twelve and a half cents for a cold bit, and twenty-five cents for a regular meal. It was the fashion in those days to purchase meals at the tavern, for the host made his profit from the liquor and the room fare, which was only ten cents for a night's lodging.

In the front room was built a great fire in the spacious fireplace, and in a semicircle around it, feet were placed before the fire and heads on their rolled up buffalo robes; here slept the tired traveler. A rheumatic tiller of the soil paid for half a bed in one of the double-bedded rooms, which all taverns then contained, and got the full bed's worth, in deep hallows and high billows of live-geese feathers, warm homespun blankets and patchwork quilts.

Of the finer quality of New Hampshire inns, many travelers testified that the host and hostesses sat at the table with you, and did the honors of a comfortable meal. Upon going away, you paid your fare without haggling. You met neatness, dignity and decency. The chambers were neat, the beds good, the sheets clean, supper passable, cider, tea, punch and all, for fourteen pence a head.

It was certainly a festive scene as coaches dashed into the inn's barn or shed, and the tired driver, after putting up his steed, walked quickly

This inn, known as the Notch House, was located in the White Mountains. This scene shows the Notch House as it was originally built in Crawford Notch. *Drawing by William H. Bartlett, circa 1836.*

to the tavern room, where sat the host behind the cage-like counter, and there ranged the inspiring barrels of old Medford or Jamaica rum and hard cider.

Members of our best and most respected families operated these taverns. These landlords were frequently magistrates, justices of the peace or sheriffs of the county. At all these local inns and taverns we would find notices of the town meetings and new laws and ordinances of administration, just as legal notices are printed in our newspapers today. Bills of sale, auctions and records of transfer were naturally posted therein. The taverns were the original places of business. It was no wonder that all men in the township flocked to the tavern; they had to know everything of town and state affairs, to say nothing of local scandals. Distances were given in almanacs of the day—not from town to town, but from tavern to tavern.

One of the most famous inns, located in Crawford Notch in the White Mountains, was the Notch House. This was a very popular stop for the traveler through the Notch. The road here is only wide enough for a single carriage, and by its side the small river is almost lost among the large granite rocks of its rugged bed. The entrance on each side is well guarded by high, steep cliffs.

In front is the bare rock known as the Elephant's Head. A footpath leads to it summit, which affords a fine view of the Notch and the surrounding scenery.

To the left, at the base of the Notch, is T.J. Crawford's well-known Notch House, as pictured. To the right of the road, which passes Notch House, is seen a part of the meadow through which winds the small Saco River, scarcely a yard in width, fed by the mountain streams boarded on either side of the Notch.

## THE VILLAGE LIVERY STABLE

Just how many of our readers remember the old village livery stable? For the benefit of those who have never heard of one, it was an establishment that catered to horses. It boarded them, doctored them and bred them whenever required. It also furnished rigs—a horse and buggy or perhaps a team—for anyone who wished to ride, rather than walk, about the village or surrounding countryside. It was a popular service for traveling men who came into town on the train and wanted to call on customers in crossroad towns. We used to hire a carriage with fringe on top and two shiny black leather seats and call on relatives in Sandwich. We brought our own buggy whip, a beautiful article of whalebone adorned with mother-of-pearl handle.

As was often the case with people in small towns during that beautiful age, the stable owner usually had side jobs. Besides being the only veterinarian in the region, he owned and drove the only hearse in town. These were low-hung carriages with doors and plate-glass windows that could be raised or lowered at will. The driver rode on an elevated seat behind the horses. They were used mostly for funerals and weddings.

The hearse was the showpiece at the stable. It had a high seat in front from which the driver proudly managed the pair of reins. Whenever the occasion arose and the hearse was in service, the driver wore a top hat, which looked like it was bought from a vaudeville supply house. To add to the illusion, there were golden tassels inside the hearse and carved cherubs at each corner. The set of harnesses was decorated with brass spots, red-white-and-blue rosettes and tall, rust-colored pompoms between the horses' ears. It seemed that the hearse driver enjoyed the

The old H. Abbott & Co. Carriage, Made & Repaired shop in Belmont. This building was located on Main Street, near the location of Penny's Market. When the building was moved here, the shop was moved to the rear, where it was used for many years before it finally burned in the early 1920s.

sense of importance as he sat with perfect dignity in the upper seat of the hearse.

Whenever a new traveler arrived at the B&M train station on the outskirts of the village, he had no trouble locating the local livery. It had its own aroma, an unmistakable blend of manure, harness oil, old and new leather, Sloan' Liniment and hay in all stages of ripeness.

On summer evenings when Mr. Cowan, the stable owner, sat out in front of his livery, the unforgettable odor of his amazing pipe dominated all other smells. This pipe was well known in the neighborhood; it was feared and respected.

Besides the regular help, there were always a number of loafers hanging around the stable. It was a favorite haunt for small boys. It was generally believed that a livery stable was second only to the poolroom as a sink of iniquity. Traveling men usually gave their stories a rehearsal at the livery before starting out on their route.

In front of the building there was a room that was partitioned off as an office. It was furnished with a littered desk, a potbellied stove, a cuspidor and half dozen wooden chairs. Tramps usually made the livery stable their first port of call when looking for a free bed. If they could convince Mr. Cowan that they wouldn't smoke or make off with one of his horses, they were allowed to sleep in the haymow or on the bales in the empty stall. Some of the more respectable gentlemen bedded down there when they knew it was dangerous to go home.

One of the major functions of a livery stable was to serve as a headquarters for horse breeding in town. In this, Mr. Cowan took an active interest. He rented box stalls to owners of stallions, who stood their animals there during the breeding season. He himself owned two jackasses. Jacks are curious beasts, given to whims and vagaries. Experienced jack keepers can spend hours telling of their idiosyncrasies. Unlike his highly bred cousin, the racehorse, a jackass cares nothing for mascots like bantam roosters, goats or Shetland ponies. He lives alone and seems to like it.

Jackasses bray when the notion strikes them. Now, Mr. Cowan's barn was made of tin. There is no sound, which is as startling as that of a jack braying in a tin barn. A good barn gives good resonance, like a good horn. If the barn is full of cracks, it will leak compression and won't carry the sound very far. In time, Mr. Cowan decided that mule breeding was falling off so much that he wouldn't replace them. A few years later his livery stable followed the jacks into oblivion. He sold it to a young fellow who wanted to start a repair shop for a new contraption called an automobile—"It'll never catch on!"

## THE COOPER SHOP

Just ask the average youngsters today what was made in a cooper shop and chances are they don't know. Yet, in certain old New Hampshire towns, more common than the village smithy was the farm cooper shop, where wooden barrels were made by hand.

Most early settlers had to learn many skills for survival; being a cooper was one such skill. Sometimes they doubled as the village smithy. As time passed, small shops appeared on the scene, most of which were near lumber mills well equipped with a workbench, a few simple tools, a frame for setting up barrels and a fireplace.

Several years ago I happened to visit such a shop and out of curiosity, I sought out the purpose of such a business. The proprietor gave me a detailed lesson that I will never forget. Now I share this lesson as related to me by Mr. Page.

It seems that the lumber used came from the nearby sawmills. The great abundance and good quality of its oak and chestnut timber led

Here Arthur page is seen working in his shop in Tamworth, New Hampshire, 1940s.

many of the citizens of the town, early in the nineteenth century, to engage in manufacture of barrels and other casks. Later, oak and chestnut thinned out and white pine was used instead.

Forest trees to be converted to lumber for barrels were marked and felled. The logs were cut in the forest into bolts the right length for staves. In the mill these bolts were sawed into staves by the cylindrical barrel saw. From other bolts the required size, barrel heads were cut and beveled, either in one piece or for some casks in several pieces.

Wooden hoops for the barrels were made from gray birch saplings an inch or two in diameter, sometimes from alder or maple. Cut to approximately the right length, they were delivered to the shop tied in bunches to be thrown into tanks containing water to soak until pliable.

Some farmers prepared hoops in the winter months. They cut their own saplings, split them, shaved them to the right thickness and tied them together for delivery to the larger shops.

Once the lumber was seasoned, the cooper trimmed the staves. It took a skilled cooper to shape a stave for a tight barrel. His work had to be accurate so that the finished barrel would be symmetrical.

Next came setting up the barrel. In a form the size of the required cask or keg, the staves were set upright. A rope was put around the staves and tightened by a windlass in order to draw them together and temporary iron hoops were fitted over the top and bottom to hold them in place.

It was now ready for permanent hoops. The first hoops adjusted were bilge hoops—one on either side of the swelling of the barrel. Quarter hoops were often used midway between the bilge and the ends of the barrel. These, after fitting, were tapped gently into place with a wedge-shaped hoop driver and cooper's hammer. The tap tap of the hammer was a customary sound heard from the shop.

Next, the stave ends were beveled and the grove for the heads cut. Once the kegs were complete they were immediately put into service. They were carefully piled on wagons with a tall and wide rigging attached and headed for the nearest depot for shipment to the coastal cities of Portsmouth, Boston, Providence, Pawtucket, New York and Philadelphia.

Some of the charm of the old villages has vanished and the musical tap tap of the cooper's hammer is no longer heard.

## A WINNIPESAUKEE STEAMBOAT EXCURSION

*First a lake tinted with sunset, next the weary lines of the receding hills.*
*—John Greenleaf Whittier.*

There is a certain romance in taking a steamboat excursion on the big lake for the first time. It was midsummer when the boat left Wolfeboro

Bay; one of those pictures, forever ineffaceable, presents itself. In effect, all the conditions are perfect for a fine Sunday afternoon sail.

Here is the shining expanse of the lake stretching away in the distance and finally lost among tufted islets and foliage-rounded promontories. To our right lay the Ossipee Mountains—dark, vigorously outlined and wooded to their summit. To our left, at a greater distance, rise the twin domes of the Belknap peaks, Gunstock and Mount Belknap. In front, and closing the view, lie the imposing Sandwich summits dominating the scene.

Having taken in the grandeur, the eye is occupied with its details. We see the lake quivering in the sunlight. From bold summit to beautiful water, the shores are clothed in most vivid green. The islands, which we believe to be floating gardens, are almost tropical in the luxuriance and richness of their vegetation. Here and there a glimmer of water through the trees denotes secluded little havens. Boats float idly on the calm surface. Waterfowl rise and beat the glossy, dark water with startled wings.

Our steamer glides swiftly and noiselessly on, attended by the echo of her paddles from the shores. Dimpled waves, parting from her bow and rolling indolently in, break on the form-fretted shores. The shore rocks give warmth of color, a pure transparency to the water, brightness to the foliage, an invigorating strength in the mountains that exert a cheerful influence upon our spirit.

Advancing up the lake, new and rare vistas rapidly succeed. Leaving Long Island, the near ranges draw apart, holding us admiring spectators of the moving panorama of distance summits. At this given point on the lake, between Five and Six Mile Islands, an opening appears through which Mount Washington bursts upon us blue as a chaplet of clouds crowning a god's imperial front. Slowly, majestically, he marches by, and now Mount Chocorua scowls upon us. A murmur of admiration runs from group to group as these monumental figures successively unveil themselves. The grandest type, which these mountains enclose, is thus displayed in the full splendor of the noonday.

Our steamer is now rapidly nearing Center Harbor. On the right its progress gradually unmasks the western slopes of the Ossipee Range, now fully opening the view of Mount Chocorua and its dependent peaks. We are now looking in the direction of Tamworth, Ossipee and Conway. Red Hill, a detached mountain at the head of the lake, moves

A majestic view of Lake Winnipesaukee as seen from the summit of Red Hill in Center Harbor. *Drawing by William H. Bartlett, 1834.*

into the gap, excluding further view of distant summits. To the west, thronged with islands, is the long reach of water toward the outlet of the lake at the Weirs.

This was the highway over which Native American war parties advanced or retreated during their predatory incursions from Canada. The Native Americans who inhabited villages at Winnipesaukee (Weirs), Ossipee and Pigwacket (Fryeburg) were hostile; from time to time during the old wars, troops were marched from the English settlements to subdue them. These scouting parties found the woods well stocked with bears, moose and deer and the lake with salmon and trout, some of which, according to the information I have, were as much as three feet long, and weighed twelve pounds each.

Traces of Native American occupation remained up to this century. Fishing weirs and woodland paths are frequently discovered today. A greater curiosity is mentioned by Dr. Jeremy Belknap in his *History of New Hampshire.* There is a story told of a pine tree standing on the shores of Winnipesaukee River, on which was carved a canoe with two men in it, supposed to have been a mark of direction to those who were expected to follow. Another was a tree in Moultonboro, standing near a carry-place between two ponds. On this tree was a representation of one of their expeditions. The number killed and the prisoners were shown by rude drawings of human beings, the former being distinguished by the mark of a knife across the throat.

We reached Center Harbor at two in the afternoon. There was still time to ascend Red Hill before sunset. This eminence would be called a mountain anywhere else. Its altitude is inconsiderable, but its location at the head of the lake, on its very borders, is highly favorable to a commanding prospect of the surrounding Lakes Region.

After a little promenade of better than an hour, we reached the summit, from which a fire watchtower stood as a sentinel to the White Mountains. Without extravagance, the view is one of the most breathtaking and engaging that the eye ever looked upon. We have before us that beautiful valley extending between the Sandwich chain on the left and the Ossipee Range on the right, the distance filled by a background of mountains. It was across this valley that we saw Mount Washington.

From this point the Sandwich Mountains take far greater interest and character. High and more distant peaks peer curiously over their brawny shoulders from their lairs in the valley of the Pemigewasset, but more remarkable, weirder than all, is the gigantic monolith that tops the rock-ribbed pile of Mount Chocorua. As the sun glides down in the west, a ruddy glow tinges its pinnacle while the shadows lurking in the ravines steal up the mountainside and crouch for a final spring upon the summit. As times passes, twilight flows over the valley and a thin haze rises from its surface.

We have waited for this moment, and now turn to the lake. Winnipesaukee is visible through its whole length, the multitude of islands peeping above it giving the idea of an inundation rather than an island sea. On the farthest shore appear mere specks of white denoting houses. So unsubstantial is the Grand Monadnock that it appears to be a fixed sentinel of all this assemblage of mountains. Glowing in sunset splendor, streaked with all the hues of the rainbow, this land is indeed magnificent.

Our imagination must assist to reproduce this ravishing spectacle. This paradise seems to have opened wide its gates to our enraptured gaze. Here we stand silent and spellbound with a strange, exquisite feeling at the heart. We feel a thrill when a voice from the forest breaks the solemn stillness of this almost supernatural vision. Our mind runs over the most striking incidents of scripture, when the sublimity of the scene is always in harmony with the grandeur of the event: the Temptation, the Sermon on the Mount, the Transfiguration. Memory brings to our aid these words, so simple, yet so expressive: "And he went up into the mountain to pray, himself, alone."

## The Rural Auctions

You won't be in the North Country long before you see a sign saying "Auction Today," or a red flag showing the way. Stop in and you just might find a relic, a fine collectable and free entertainment. I've always enjoyed a good country auction, for it unites the best features of the church social, country fair, an old-fashioned lawn party and, most important, the Yankee trader and treasure hunter. Given a good auctioneer, who must have a theatrical approach to the selling of old anvils or priceless paintings, the visitor is assured of an entertaining afternoon.

Usually these affairs are held in a large open tent or barn (bring your own folding chair), or possibly in a rented hall. The auction is an "open sesame" to the country people, its lingo and its wealth of antique and collectable furniture and gadgets.

Listen to the auctioneer as he sings out, "Here's a fine Dalton pitcher, folks. Let's start it at fifty. Do I hear fifty? Start me at twenty-five! Speak right up! Good. Who'll say thirty? I hear the music of thirty, forty, now fifty, sixty. Sixty once, sixty twice! Are you done at sixty? Sold! A good buy that is for sixty dollars."

Sometimes a couple of local dowagers will get to bidding against each other for an old mohair sofa or a Queen Anne chair. Their rivalry spices the afternoon with drama and humor.

Auctions may get to be habit-forming, for good buys are to be had. You visit one and just missed out on a genuine old cobbler's bench that you craved for a coffee table. But something better might turn up at the next auction. There, you bid on a couple of wooden sap buckets and a three-legged milk stool.

A word to the wise: There are two basic rules that the novice auction follower should observe. Don't overbid, and don't bid on anything you can't carry away in your car or van. I know of a case where a gentleman bought an Italian urn for thirty dollars. It was made of granite and

A country auction in Sandwich, New Hampshire, 1930s.

weighed several hundred pounds. It cost him plenty to have it delivered to his home. "AUCTION TODAY—FOLLOW THE SIGNS!"

## FAIR TIME IN NEW HAMPSHIRE

### SANDWICH FAIR—1800S

It was a long ride from our mountain home to Sandwich, with one horse and the two-seater democrat wagon full.

It was a beautiful day in October—the sun rising in a slight haze on our far eastern view, and the air chilled by an evening frost. Morning chores were hurried with the excitement of the forthcoming day, and by seven-thirty, the horse was hitched and ready to travel. An ample lunch, packed in great-grandma's round, wooden butter boxes, was stored under the seats, and we in starched gingham were seated prim and quiet. In a full democrat there was no extra space and the children in those days had to sit still.

Down the mountain road the horse trotted rhythmically. Leaves were just beginning to turn color and along the roadside were the purple-frosted flowers, and here and there the aroma of wild grapes.

Soon we arrived at Center Harbor and onto the Bean Road along the shoreline of Squam Lake.

As we approached Center Sandwich we saw that there would be many strangers there. On all the roads and crossroads, buggies and democrats, carryalls and farm wagons were all going to the fair; even our horse seemed to catch the excitement and trotted briskly along the level way. Soon the fairgrounds came into view and the high board fence and the roofs of the big exhibition halls were clearly visible. Then we were there and father was getting the tickets.

With a stream of other vehicles we went directly into the grounds and found a place with other teams inside the high fence. Their horses were unhitched from wagons and haltered to hitching rings. It was by then a little past ten in the morning. In a close family group we walked over to the midway. Here were the wonders we had come to see, the half-awesome mystery of the sideshow tents. There was a fortune teller who would read your palm or gaze for you into a crystal ball, and, of course, there was the wild man from Borneo.

Outside the tents there were barkers crying the wonders of their show, strange-looking men dressed in very strange clothes. Walking beside them was exciting enough without going inside the tent; it was like being in some far-off land of our geography book. At one tent, glittering brass cymbals flashed in the sunlight, while at another, tambourines jangled in the hands of a dancer. From one side of the midway the merry-go-round whirled to the rhythmic tune of the steam calliope.

We didn't ride the merry-go-round; Mother was afraid "we might get dizzy and fall off." We didn't ride the Ferris wheel either, because "it might get stuck and couldn't get down." However, we did stroll over to the livestock stables to view the hogs and hens.

Mother insisted that we go to the exhibition hall and see the prize quilts and rugs. The building's roof was higher than Grandpa's barn, and all around were hung many beautiful quilts. Some of these quilts were made of tiny squares, while others were like flower gardens. With the quilts were many rugs—braided, crocheted and hooked. How many hours of patient work went into their making! Long winter hours in the farm kitchen when the road was piled with snow, long winter evenings with the kerosene lamp on the pine table, Father reading *Farm and Home*, the children playing dominoes, Mother sewing patchwork and now the quilts and rugs are proudly displayed at the fair.

A horse-pulling contest at Sandwich Fair in the 1940s.

Around the hall there were showcases of glittering cheap jewelry, beads and pins, tables of souvenir knickknacks, little fluted vases and small cups and pin-trays with "Sandwich Fair" stamped on them. From the main hall we went on to the displays of home-canned pickles, fruit and jelly. There were large, delicious-smelling apples—red and green—and all kinds of vegetables, huge yellow pumpkins and mammoth squashes. Here we joined Father and left the great hall to look at the cattle in the long sheds and went to the poultry house to see the pert highbred roosters and hens, White Leghorns, Plymouth Rocks, Buff Cochins, sprightly game cocks and diminutive Bantams.

Presently it was noon. We returned to the wagon, spread a horse blanket on the ground and gladly sat down to a box lunch of homemade bread and butter, new pickles, cold roast chicken, pumpkin pie, chocolate frosted cake and big molasses cookies. Many friends and relatives dropped by to chat with my parents; folks they hadn't seen for years from Strafford, Barnstead, Farmington and as far away as Laconia and Meredith. It was fun being at the fair.

After lunch we leisurely strolled around the grounds. An amusing sight for us was the organ grinder, a small, dark-skinned man with a big mustache. Then there was a man selling balloons and little whips. Father bought a red balloon and a tiny horsewhip for me. From the peanut vendor he bought a multi-colored bag of peanuts in their shells; they were still very warm from the roaster.

Let us not forget the Grand Street Parade with prancing horses, cattle of every description, the smart sounding town bands, colorful school, Grange and church floats. There were old fancy democrats polished to the tee. What a grand parade.

Finally, it was time for the balloon ascension. While father was hitching up the horse for our departure, we watched them soar through the air as we left the fairgrounds. Most of the other people were starting for home, also. As we streamed away from the fairgrounds, the road was filled with buggies and wagons, but as we approached the crossroad at Center Harbor, only two were in sight. How quiet our mountain road seemed as the horse slowly climbed the last long hill in the twilight of the shortening October day! In our far view we could look away off toward Center Sandwich.

Yes, this one-day fair is still providing entertainment for the young and old alike. And yes, the vendors are still barking their wares and the fine exhibits may still be seen, as well as cattle pulling contests. The fairs are still a tradition in New Hampshire and a fine place to reminisce and meet new friends.

## Early New Hampshire Quakers

During the turn of the nineteenth century, there were a considerable number of remarkable Christians called Friends, or Quakers. This interesting denomination of Christians may be entitled to a brief notice, as their practice seemed an exemplification of the moral law and the faith that was in them, as well as their simplification of the freedom, protection and restraint sought to be accorded by government.

Quakers are sometimes confounded with Shakers, who are totally different except in the plainness and simplicity of demeanor, language and dress, and the precepts of their creed. Like most of the other sects, Quakers encouraged and believed in the sacred character of marriage and family relations, honesty and efficient civil government, trade, business and accumulating and devising property.

According to their personal discipline, "We have, as a people, looked upon ourselves as well as the primitive Christians to be included in the notable prophecy of Isaiah II, 4: 'They shall beat

The Quaker Meetinghouse in North Sandwich near Whiteface Mountain.

their swords into plowshars and their spears into pruning-hooks, and learn to war no more.'"

It was most evident that war or bearing arms for any purpose was forbidden, and as consistency was claimed to be one of their brightest jewels, they objected to the payment of taxes for any such purpose, but suffered them to be collected, owing to their nonresistant principles. Such goods as are not self-sustaining were provided for by the society, all funds being raised by voluntary subscription; consequently no poorhouses were maintained by them or among them and squalid poverty was even less frequent among them than immense wealth. Both were rare.

During the middle of the nineteenth century there were about twenty meetinghouses in the state, and though they did not increase in number and influence, as did other denominations, still they maintained the even tenor of their ways, and may serve as a profitable example to all of us.

One such meetinghouse still stands today east of the Durgin Covered Bridge in North Sandwich, New Hampshire.

## THE CHURCH SUPPER

The church mouse did not achieve his legendary reputation for leanness by mere accident. He was no doubt the inhabitant of a country church in the days of our fathers (grandfathers), when he sometimes ran a poor second to the minister. Now I'm dating myself, for I well remember those Saturday evening church suppers (socials) during the forties.

The often-underpaid ministers to the souls of our rural forefathers were often reduced to a polite form of begging, and few of their families rose above genteel under-nourishment. Their parishioners had no illusion about how much food and clothing the eighty or a hundred dollars a year would buy. The customary supplement to this starvation wage was the church social, given as a benefit for the parson and his family.

Church socials were held on the lawn of the church on summer evenings. Members of the church donated cake, platters of fried chicken, canned preserves, fruit and other delicacies of the season, which were served at plank tables and laid on wooden sawhorses. Food was served family style and the usual cost of a church social meal was twenty-five cents for all you could eat. Ten cents was charged for children, who usually ate twice as much as the adults. The leaders of the community presided at the cake table, where the work was easy and they got a chance to compare the baking skill of their neighbors. The parson's wife and members of the congregation washed dishes and served the hot food from a brick stove or kerosene range set up for the evening under a canvas. It was a gala time for the children of the town who could play on this rare occasion when neither Sunday school nor public school cast a shadow on their spirits.

The minister's family was richer by twenty-five or thirty dollars, everybody had a good time and the housewife gathered up enough leftovers to feed her family the next day, a phenomenon of the fish and loaves sort that was very mysterious and wonderful.

Today, church suppers are still a social tradition in the community, hopefully for a different purpose.

The Old Meetinghouse Baptist Church in Sandwich Village. This edifice was built in 1793.

## Christmas

When I was young, Christmas in New Hampshire had a quality about it not found elsewhere. Our isolation and simple life on the farm gave it special importance, a special kind of observance. Santa Claus made his visit and he brought us simple but highly prized gifts. But in our country village, Christmas was not primarily a time for gift giving; the big event of the season was a family reunion.

The elaborate preparation for the reunion started in late fall with a round of letters from distant kinfolk who would return to the ancestral homes there in the hills for the magic season.

To the boys of the family fell the chore of getting in a good wood supply. We did that on Saturdays when out of school, for we didn't want to be bothered with that when the holidays came. In addition to plenty of small, dry wood for the cookstove, we also needed a lot of green, long-burning wood for the fireplace. All-day wood made too hot a fire and burned up too quickly. A generous sprinkling of fresh green hardwood lasted longer and it sizzled and sang as it burned. A lot of the big backlogs were essential, so we wouldn't have to put on wood so often. A cord of wood was stacked in the sheltered end of the porch, handy and dry for the women in the kitchen.

The first big event of the season was the closing of school for the holidays. When that came we knew the glorious days were now at hand. On the last day, we took the teacher homemade presents and in return she gave each of us little bags of fruit and candy. That last day was long, but finally we heard the magic word, "dismissed," and we ran from the room calling "Merry Christmas" to the teacher, as she put out the dying fire in the big Franklin stove.

The group became smaller and smaller as the paths divided up the valley and over the ridge, and at last we were home. Two delightful weeks lay ahead. We put our books away, pulled off our school clothes and put on our everyday clothes. That was the perfect moment, when everything was right with the world.

We eagerly watched for the mailman every day. We waited for his vehicle to round the bend below, informing us when the clan would gather.

About that time we'd butcher, too. The thrifty New Englanders of our valley knew how to make many good things from a pig; those who had drifted to far places were especially hungry for the real pig roast. Nowhere else in the valley did it taste the same. The perfect seasonings were added so as to keep well and improve with age.

For a variety, hens and a goose were fattened in a coop, and the big turkey was destined for the Christmas table. Every meal during Christmas week was a big one, but the table groaned on Christmas

Day. There would be a turkey and several other kinds of meat—both fresh and cured—every kind of vegetable possible, two or three kinds of pies, two or three kinds of cakes. The young people would eat until no more would go down. Food was pretty rich, and we weren't accustomed to that. For a long time after Christmas week we craved the simpler things. The day after our last company left, we waded into a pot of baked potatoes and then we would vary that with peas and golden corn bread. Those things went well together, and our parents told us they were easy on the stomach and good for what ailed us.

As fine as the days were, nights were even finer. Then we all met at the ancestral home, known to all as the House. After the evening meal we all took the winding path to the House. On old maps, the House was shown as Ladd's Tavern. It was there the stagecoaches stopped during the earlier days and travelers from what was the frontier then across the mountains in New Hampshire were put up for the night.

The living room was not crowded, even when the whole family gathered. At the east end was an enormous fireplace, the only source of heat, but ample enough to make the large room comfortable. The setback table was placed in the center of the room. There the gambling element of the clan had a spirited game of cards every night, often into the small hours. There was much teasing and joking, all in good humor. The women sat in a large circle around the wall and small talked with the others. Most of them had embroidery, quilt patches or other needlework that kept their unconscious hands busy, while their tongues wagged.

The kids played on the floor between the circle of women and the card group in the center. Most of the time we were teasing to go out and shoot firecrackers, which for some reason was a part of the Christmas tradition. One of the men brought a shovel full of burning embers from the fireplace and put them in a little pile in the red clay yard. There, we kids shot a few of our precious firecrackers at night. I remember how much fun it was to chase each other with Roman candles, shooting sizzling balls of fire at our companions as they scurried all over the yard and took refuge down behind the woodpile.

One night during Christmas week was set aside for Christmas exercises at the church. That was when we kids showed off. Our teachers and parents coached us for weeks in our little pieces of songs. We always had a large cedar or holly tree that filled one corner of the

Gathering together around the open hearth to celebrate the holiday are family, friends and relatives. Note the two young people sitting in the fireplace.

church. On it were draped long strands of bright red holly berries and popcorn that we strung for that purpose. They were the only tree ornaments we knew.

Each day had its own special event, but Christmas morning was the one that reached the peak of excitement and anticipation. Our parents got up before dawn on Christmas morning and made a roaring fire and then called us. We were dressed and ready, huddled quietly on the stairway.

Our gifts were mostly of the useful kind—knitted socks, gloves, scarves and sweaters. There might be a homemade rag doll for the younger girls and a few ten-cent presents from the variety store near the village. Ten cents would buy a pocketknife or a doll that would cost at least twenty dollars now. Sometimes gifts were ordered from Sears. My folks once ordered a knife for me, the most treasured possession I ever had.

All too soon the magic week was over. Each day after New Year's our group grew smaller. Upon their departure, there was much kissing, hugging, waving goodbyes and yelling words of parting to those returning to distant parts.

Christmas was over. We faced school again the next day, and a bleakness that looked like eternity before the magic season could come again. The new calendar was hung on the wall and *Leavitt's Almanac* from the nail on the edge of the mantel there over the kitchen stove. Both of them looked mighty sad with Christmas covered by eleven deadly pages!

# Selected Bibliography


Anderson, Earl. *Farm House.* 1877.

Andrew, Henry N. "The Royal Pine." *Appalachia* 27, no. 2 (1948).

*Ballou's Pictorial Drawing Room Companion*. Boston: 1855.

Batchelder, John N. *Popular Resorts*. Boston: Batchelder Publishing, 1874.

Belknap, Jeremy. *History of New Hampshire*. Dover: Hampshire Publisher, 1862.

Bisbee, Ernest E. *The White Mountain Scrapbook.* Lancaster: 1946.

Browne, George W., ed. *Granite Monthly* 1, Concord: 1907.

Daniel, Gene. *White Mountain Guide*. 26 ed. Boston: Appalachian Mountain Club, 1998.

Daughters of the American Revolution (Mary Butler Chapter). *Old Meredith & Vicinity*. Laconia: 1926.

Drake, Samuel. *The Heart of the Mountains*. New York: Harpers and Brothers, 1882.

Greene, William H. *Geneva Point Center*. 1989.

Heald, Bruce D. *Follow the Mount*. Winnipesaukee Flagship Corporation, 1971.

———. *Steamboats in Motion*. Winnipesaukee Flagship Corporation, 1980.

Hill, Ruth. "The Fair," *New Hampshire Profile*. 1955.

Kilbourne, Frederick W. *Chronicles of the White Mountains.* Boston: 1916.

King, Starr. *The White Mountains*. Boston: Crosby and Ainsworth, 1866.

Manning, Robert E., ed. "Mountain Passages." *Appalachia Anthology*. 1982.

McClintock, John N. *New Hampshire History.* Concord Press, 1889.

McGinnis, R.J., ed. *The Good Old Days*. New York: Harper Brothers, 1960.

Metcalf, H.H. *Granite Monthly*. 13, Concord: 1894.

O'Kane, Walter C. *Trails & Summits of the White Mountains*. 1925.

Okes, William. *White Mountain Scenery*. Ipswich, MA: 1848.

Oppel, Frank. *Tales of Yesterday's New England*. Secaucus, NJ: Castle Publishing Co., 1989.

Pillsbury, Hobart. *New Hampshire History*. New York: Lewis Historical Publishing Company, 1927.

Robinson, William F. *Abandoned New England*. Boston: New York Graphic Society, 1978.

Spaulding, James W. "Memory Barn." *New Hampshire Profile,* 1967.

Speare, Mrs. Guy E. *New Hampshire Folk Tales*. Brattleboro, VT: Stephen Daye Press, 1936.

Stone, Mary I. *Winter Breakfast*. 1957.

Sweetser, Moses F., ed. *The White Mountains: A Handbook for Travelers*. Boston: J.R. Osgood, 1884.

Thompson, Betty F., ed. *The Changing Face of New England*. 1958.

Tolles, Bryant F., Jr. *The Grand Resort Hotels in the White Mountains*. Boston: David R. Godine, 1998.

www.ingramcontent.com/pod-product-compliance
Lightning Source LLC
LaVergne TN
LVHW052342100826
845147LV00021B/1153